My First Book

My First Book

Various

MINT EDITIONS

My First Book was first published in 1897.

This edition published by Mint Editions 2021.

ISBN 9781513291802 | E-ISBN 9781513294650

Published by Mint Editions®

 MINT
EDITIONS

minteditionbooks.com

Publishing Director: Jennifer Newens
Design & Production: Rachel Lopez Metzger
Project Manager: Micaela Clark
Typesetting: Westchester Publishing Services

Contents

Introduction

By Jerome K. Jerome

P lease, sir," he said, "could you tell me the right time?"

"Twenty minutes to eight," I replied, looking at my watch.

"Oh," he remarked. Then added for my information after a pause: "I haven't got to be in till half-past eight."

After that we fell back into our former silence, and sat watching the murky twilight, he at his end of the park seat, I at mine.

"And do you live far away?" I asked, lest, he having miscalculated, the short legs might be hard put to it.

"Oh no, only over there," he answered, indicating with a sweep of his arm the northern half of London where it lay darkening behind the chimney-fringed horizon; "I often come and sit here."

It seemed an odd pastime for so very small a citizen. "And what makes you like to come and sit here?" I said.

"Oh, I don't know," he replied, "I think."

"And what do you think about?"

"Oh—oh, lots of things."

He inspected me shyly out of the corner of his eye, but, satisfied apparently by the scrutiny, he sidled up a little nearer.

"Mama does not like this evening time," he confided to me; "it always makes her cry. But then," he went on to explain, "Mama has had a lot of trouble, and that makes anyone feel different about things, you know."

I agreed that this was so. "And do you like this evening time?" I enquired.

"Yes," he answered; "don't you?"

"Yes, I like it too," I admitted. "But tell me why you like it, then I will tell you why I like it."

"Oh," he replied, "things come to you."

"What things?" I asked.

Again his critical eye passed over me, and it raised me in my own conceit to find that again the inspection contented him, he evidently feeling satisfied that here was a man to whom another gentleman might speak openly and without reserve.

He wriggled sideways, slipping his hands beneath him and sitting on them.

"Oh, fancies," he explained; "I'm going to be an author when I grow up, and write books."

Then I knew why it was that the sight of his little figure had drawn me out of my path to sit beside him, and why the little serious face had seemed so familiar to me, as of someone I had once known long ago.

So we talked of books and bookmen. He told me how, having been born on the fourteenth of February, his name had come to be Valentine, though privileged parties, as for example Aunt Emma, and Mr. Dawson, and Cousin Naomi, had shortened it to Val, and Mama would sometimes call him Pickaniny, but that was only when they were quite alone. In return I confided to him my name, and discovered that he had never heard it, which pained me for the moment, until I found that of all my confrères, excepting only Mr. Stevenson, he was equally ignorant, he having lived with the heroes and the heroines of the past, the new man and the new woman, the new pathos and the new humour being alike unknown to him.

Scott and Dumas and Victor Hugo were his favourites. "Gulliver's Travels," "Robinson Crusoe," "Don Quixote," and the "Arabian Nights," he knew almost by heart, and these we discussed, exchanging many pleasant and profitable ideas upon the same. But the psychological novel, I gathered, was not to his taste. He liked "*real* stories," he told me, naïvely unconscious of the satire, "where people did things."

"I used to read silly stuff once," he confessed humbly, "Indian tales and that sort of thing, you know, but Mama said I'd never be able to write if I read that rubbish."

"So you gave it up," I concluded for him.

"Yes," he answered. But a little sigh of regret, I thought, escaped him at the same time.

"And what do you read now?" I asked.

"I'm reading Marlowe's plays and De Quincey's Confessions (he called him Quinsy) just now," was his reply.

"And do you understand them?" I queried.

"Fairly well," he answered. Then added more hopefully, "Mama says I'll get to like them better as I go on."

"I want to learn to write very, very well indeed," he suddenly added after a long pause, his little earnest face growing still more serious, "then I'll be able to earn heaps of money."

It rose to my lips to answer him that it was not always the books written very, very well that brought in the biggest heaps of money; that if heaps of money were his chiefest hope he would be better advised to devote his energies to the glorious art of self-advertisement and the gentle craft of making friends upon the Press. But something about the almost baby face beside me, fringed by the gathering shadows, silenced my middle-aged cynicism. Involuntarily my gaze followed his across the strip of foot-worn grass, across the dismal-looking patch of ornamental water, beyond the haze of tangled trees, beyond the distant row of stuccoed houses, and, arrived there with him, I noticed many men and women clothed in the garments of all ages and all lands, men and women who had written very, very well indeed and who notwithstanding had earned heaps of money, the hire worthy of the labourer, and who were not ashamed; men and women who had written true words which the common people had read gladly; men and women who had been raised to lasting fame upon the plaudits of their day; and before the silent faces of these, made beautiful by Time, the little bitter sneers I had counted truth rang foolish in my heart, so that I returned with my young friend to our green seat beside the foot-worn grass, feeling by no means so sure as when I had started which of us twain were the better fitted to teach wisdom to the other.

"And what would you do, Valentine, with heaps of money?" I asked.

Again for a moment his old shyness of me returned. Perhaps it was not quite a legitimate question from a friend of such recent standing. But his frankness wrestled with his reserve and once more conquered.

"Mama need not do any work then," he answered. "She isn't really strong enough for it, you know," he explained, "and I'd buy back the big house where she used to live when she was a little girl, and take her back to live in the country—the country air is so much better for her, you know—and Aunt Emma, too."

But I confess that as regards Aunt Emma his tone was not enthusiastic.

I spoke to him—less dogmatically than I might have done a few minutes previously, and I trust not discouragingly—of the trials and troubles of the literary career, and of the difficulties and disappointments awaiting the literary aspirant, but my croakings terrified him not.

"Mama says that every work worth doing is difficult," he replied, "and that it doesn't matter what career we choose there are difficulties and disappointments to be overcome, and that I must work very hard and say to myself 'I *will* succeed,' and then in the end, you know, I shall."

"Though of course it may be a long time," he added cheerfully.

Only one thing in the slightest daunted him, and that was the weakness of his spelling.

"And I suppose," he asked, "you must spell very well indeed to be an author."

I explained to him, however, that this failing was generally met by a little judicious indistinctness of caligraphy, and all obstacles thus removed, the business of a literary gent seemed to him an exceptionally pleasant and joyous one.

"Mama says it is a noble calling," he confided to me, "and that anyone ought to be very proud and glad to be able to write books, because they give people happiness and make them forget things, and that one ought to be awfully good if one's going to be an author, so as to be worthy to help and teach others."

"And do you try to be awfully good, Valentine?" I enquired.

"Yes," he answered; "but it's awfully hard, you know. I don't think anybody could ever be *quite* good—until," he corrected himself, "they were grown up."

"I suppose," he added with a little sigh, "it's easy for grown-up people to be good."

It was my turn to glance suspiciously at him, this time wondering if the seeds of satire could have taken root already in that tiny brain. But his eyes met mine without flinching, and I was not loath to drift away from the point.

"And what else does your Mama say about literature, Valentine?" I asked. For the strangeness of it was that, though I kept repeating under my breath "Copy-book maxims, copy-book maxims," hoping by such shibboleth to protect myself from their influence, the words yet stirred within me old childish thoughts and sentiments that I, in my cleverness, had long since learnt to laugh at, and had thought forgotten. I, with my years of knowledge and experience behind me, seemed for the nonce to be sitting with Valentine at the feet of this unseen lady, listening, as I again told myself, to "copy-book maxims" and finding in them in spite of myself a certain element of truth, a certain amount of helpfulness, an unpleasant suggestion of reproach.

He tucked his hands underneath him, as before, and sat swinging his short legs.

"Oh—oh lots of things," he answered vaguely.

"Yes?" I persisted.

"Oh, that—" he repeated it slowly, recalling it word for word as he went on, "that he who can write a great book is greater than a king; that a good book is better than a good sermon; that the gift of being able to write is given to anybody in trust, and that an author should never forget that he is God's servant."

I thought of the chatter of the clubs, and could not avoid a smile. But the next moment something moved me to take his hand in mine, and, turning his little solemn face towards mine, to say:

"If ever there comes a time, little man, when you are tempted to laugh at your mother's old-fashioned notions—and such a time may come—remember that an older man than you once told you he would that he had always kept them in his heart, he would have done better work."

Then growing frightened at my own earnestness, as we men do, deeming it, God knows why, something to be ashamed of, I laughed away his answering questions, and led the conversation back to himself.

"And have you ever tried writing anything?" I asked him.

Of course he had, what need to question! And it was, strange to say, a story about a little boy who lived with his mother and aunt, and who went to school.

"It is sort of," he explained, "sort of auto—bio—graphical, you know."

"And what does Mama think of it?" was my next question, after we had discussed the advantages of drawing upon one's own personal experiences for one's material.

"Mama thinks it is very clever—in parts," he told me.

"You read it to her?" I suggested.

"Yes," he acknowledged, "in the evening, when she's working, and Aunt Emma isn't there."

The room rose up before me, I could see the sweet-faced lady in her chair beside the fire, her white hands moving to and from the pile of sewing by her side, the little flushed face of the lad bending over his pages written in sprawling schoolboy hand. I saw the love light in her eyes as every now and then she stole a covert glance across at him, I heard his childish treble rising and falling, as his small finger moved slowly down the sheet.

Suddenly it said, a little more distinctly:

"Please, sir, could you tell me the time?"

"Just over the quarter, Valentine," I answered, waking up and looking at my watch.

He rose and held out his hand.

"I didn't know it was so late," he said, "I must go now."

But as our hands met another question occurred to him.

"Oh," he exclaimed, "you said you'd tell me why you liked to come and sit here of an evening, like I do. Why?"

"So I did, Valentine," I replied, "but I've changed my mind. When you are a big man, as old as I am, you come and sit here and you'll know. But it isn't so pleasant a reason as yours, Valentine, and you wouldn't understand it. Goodnight."

He raised his cap with an old-fashioned courtesy and trotted off, looking however a little puzzled. Some distance down the path, he turned and waved his hand to me, and I watched him disappear into the twilight.

I sat on for a while, thinking many thoughts, until across the rising mist there rang a hoarse, harsh cry, "All out, All out," and slowly I moved homeward.

"Ready Money Mortiboy"

By Walter Besant

Not the very first. That, after causing its writer labour infinite, hope exaggerated, and disappointment dire, was consigned, while still in manuscript, to the flames. My little experience, however, with this work of Art, which never saw the light, may help others to believe, what is so constantly denied, that publishers *do* consider MSS. sent to them. My MS. was sent anonymously, without any introduction, through a friend. It was not only read—and refused—but it was read very conscientiously and right through. So much was proved by the reader's opinion, which not only showed the reasons—good and sufficient reasons—why he could not recommend the manuscript to be published, but also contained, indirectly, certain hints and suggestions, which opened up new ideas as to the Art of Fiction, and helped to put a strayed sheep in the right way. Now it is quite obvious that what was done for me must be constantly and consistently done for others. My very first novel, therefore, was read and refused. Would that candidates for literary honours could be made to understand that refusal is too often the very best thing that can happen to them! But the gods sometimes punish man by granting his prayers. How heavy may be the burden laid upon the writer by his first work! If anyone, for instance, should light upon the first novels written by Richard Jefferies, he will understand the weight of that burden.

My first MS., therefore, was destined to get burned or somehow destroyed. For some years it lay in a corner—say, sprawled in a corner—occupying much space. At dusk I used to see a strange, wobbling, amorphous creature in that corner among those papers. His body seemed not made for his limbs, nor did these agree with each other, and his head was out of proportion to the rest of him. He sat upon the pile of papers, and he wept, wringing his hands. "Alas!" he said: "Not another like me. Don't make another like me. I could not endure another like myself." Finally, the creature's reproaches grew intolerable; so I threw the bundle of papers behind the fire, and he vanished. One had discovered by this time that for the making even of a tolerable novel it is necessary to leave off copying other people, to observe on your own account, to study realities, to get out of the conventional groove, to rely upon one or other of the great emotions of human nature, and to try to hold the reader by dramatic presentation rather than by talk. I do not say that this discovery came all at once, but it came gradually, and it proved valuable.

One more point. A second assertion is continually being heard concerning editors. It is said that they do not read contributions offered to them. When editors publicly advertise that they do not invite contributions, or that they will not return contributions, it is reasonable to suppose that they do not read them. Well, you have heard my first experience with a publisher. Hear next an experience with editors. It is, first, to the fact that contributions *are* read by editors that I owe my introduction to James Rice and my subsequent collaboration with him. It was, next, to an unsolicited contribution that I owed a connection of many years with a certain monthly magazine. It was, lastly, through an unsolicited contribution that I became and continued for sometime a writer of leading articles for a great London daily. Therefore, when I hear that editors will not read contributions, I ask if things have changed in twenty years—and why?

I sent a paper, then, unasked, and without introduction, to the editor of *Once a Week*. The editor read it, accepted it, and sent it to the press. Immediately afterwards he left the journal because it was sold to Rice, then a young man, not long from Cambridge, and just called to the Bar. He became editor as well as proprietor. The former editor forgot to tell his successor anything about my article. Rice, finding it in type, and not knowing who had written it, inserted it shortly after he took over the journal, so that the first notice that I received that the paper was accepted was when I saw it in the magazine, bristling with printer's errors. Of course I wrote indignantly to the editor. I received a courteous reply begging me to call. I did so, and the matter was explained. Then for a year or two I continued to send things to *Once a Week*. But the paper was anything but prosperous. Indeed, I believe there was never anytime during its existence of twenty years when it could be called prosperous. After three years of gallant struggle, Rice concluded to give it up. He sold the paper. He would never confess how much he lost over it; but the ambition to become proprietor and editor of a popular weekly existed no longer in his bosom, and he was wont to grow thoughtful in after years when this episode was recalled to his memory. During this period, however, I saw a great deal of the management, and was admitted behind the scenes, and saw several remarkable and interesting people. For instance, there was a certain literary hack, a pure and simple hack, who was engaged at a salary to furnish so many columns a week to order. He was clever, something of a scholar, something of a poet, and could write a very readable paper on almost any subject. In fact, he was not in the least proud, and would undertake anything that was proposed. It was not his duty to suggest, nor did he show the least interest in his work, nor had he the least desire to advance himself. In most cases, I believe, he simply "conveyed" the matter; and if the thing was found out, he would be the first to deplore that he had "forgotten the quotes." He was a thirsty soul; he had no enthusiasm except for drink; he lived, in fact, only for drink; in order to get more money for drink he lived in one squalid room, and went in rags. One day he dismissed himself after an incident over which we may drop a veil. Sometime after it was reported that he was attempting the stage as a pantomime super. But fate fell upon him; he became ill; he was carried to a hospital; and pneumonia opened for him the gates of the other world. He was made for better things.

Again, it was in the editor's small back room that I made the acquaintance of a young lady named Julia, whose biography I afterwards related. She was a bookbinder's accountant all the day, and in the evening she was a *figurante* at one of the theatres. I think she was not a very pretty girl, but she had good eyes—of the soft, sad kind, which seem to belong to those destined to die young; and in the evening, when she was dressed, she looked very well indeed, and was placed in the front.

To the editor's office came in multitudes seedy and poverty-stricken literary men; there were not, twenty-four years ago, so many literary women as at present, but there were many more seedy literary men, because in those days the great doors of journalism were neither so wide nor so wide open as they are now. Everyone, I remember, wanted to write a series of articles. Each in turn proposed a series as if it was a new and striking idea. A certain airy, rollicking, red-nosed person, who had once walked the hospitals, proposed, I remember, to "catch science on the Wing—on the Wing, sir"—in a series of articles; a heavy, conscientious person, also red-nosed, proposed, in a series of articles, to set the world right in Economics; an irresponsible, fluttering, elderly gentleman, with a white waistcoat and a red nose, thought that a series of articles on—say the Vestries of our Native Land, would prove enormously popular; if not the Vestries, then the Question of Education, or of Emigration, or—or—something else. The main point with all was not the subject, but the series. As it happened, nobody ever was allowed to contribute a series at all. Then there were the people who sent up articles, and especially the poor ladies who were on the point of starving. Would the editor only—only take their article? Heavens! what has become of all these ladies? It was twenty-four years ago; these particular ladies must have perished long since; but there are more— and more—and more—still starving, as every editor knows full well.

Sometimes, sitting in that sanctum, I looked through their MSS. for them. Sometimes the writers called in person, and the editor had to see them, and if they were women, they went away crying, though he was always as kind as possible. Poor things! Yet what could one do? Their stuff was too—too terrible.

Another word as to the contributions. In most cases a glance at the first page was sufficient. The MS. was self-condemned. "Oh!" says the contributor; "if the editor would only tell me what is wrong, I would alter it." Dear contributor, no editor has time for teaching. You must send him the paper complete, finished, and ready for press; else it either goes back or lies on the shelf. When Rice handed over the paper to his successor, there were piles of MSS. lying on all the shelves. Where are those MSS. now? To be sure, I do not believe there was one among them all worth having.

Rice wrote a novel by himself, for his own paper. It was a work which he did not reproduce, because there were certain chapters which he wished to re-write. He was always going to re-write these chapters, but never did, and the work remains still in the columns of *Once a Week*, where it may be hunted out by those who are curious. One day, when he was lamenting the haste with which he had been compelled to send off a certain instalment, he told me that he had an idea of another novel, which seemed to him not only possible, but hopeful. He proposed that we should take up this idea together, work it out, if it approved itself to me as it did to him, and write a novel upon it together.

His idea, in the first crude form, was simple—so simple that I wonder it had never occurred to anybody before. The prodigal son was to come home again—apparently repentant—really with the single intention of feigning repentance and getting what he could out of the old man and then going back to his old companions. That was the first germ.

When we came to hammer this out together, a great many modifications became necessary. The profligate, stained with vice, the companion of scoundrels, his conscience hardened and battered and reckless, had yet left, hitherto undiscovered, some human weakness. By this weakness he had to be led back to the better life. Perhaps you have read the story, dear reader. One may say without boasting that it attracted some attention from the outset I even believe that it gave an upward turn—a last gasp—to the circulation of the dying paper.

When—to anticipate a little—the time came for publishing it, we were faced with the fact that a new and anonymous novel is naturally regarded with doubt by publishers. Nothing seems more risky than such a venture. On the other hand, we were perfectly satisfied that there was no risk in our novel at all. This, of course, we had found out, not only from the assurances of Vanity, but also from the reception the work had met with during its progress through the magazine. Therefore, we had it printed and bound at our own expense, and we placed the book, ready for publication, in the hands of Mr. William Tinsley. We so arranged the business that the printer's bill was not due till the first returns came from the publisher. By this artful plan we avoided paying anything at all. We had only printed a modest edition of 600, and these all went off, leaving, of course, a very encouraging margin. The cheap edition was sold to Henry S. King & Co. for a period of five years. Then the novel was purchased outright by Chatto & Windus, who still continue to publish it—and, I believe, to sell it. As things go, a novelist has reason to be satisfied with an immortality which stretches beyond the twenty-first year.

In another place I am continually exhorting young writers never to pay for production. It may be said that I broke my own rule.

But it will be observed that this case was not one in which production was "paid for," in the ordinary sense of the term—it was one of publication on commission of a book concerning which, we were quite certain, there was neither doubt nor risk. And this is a very good way indeed to publish, provided you have such a book, and provided your publisher will push the book with as much vigour as his own.

Now, since the origin of the story cannot be claimed as my own, I may be allowed to express an opinion upon it.

The profligate, with his dreadful past behind him, dragging him down; the low woman whom he has married; the gambler, his associate; the memory of robbery and of prison; and with the new influences around him—the girl he loves, pure and sweet, and innocent; the boy whom he picks out of the gutter; the wreck of his old father—form together a group which I have always thought to be commanding, strong, attractive, interesting, much beyond any in the ordinary run of fiction. The central figure, which, I repeat, is not my own, but my partner's initial conception, has been imitated since—in fiction and on the stage—which shows how strong he is. I do not venture to give an opinion upon the actual presentment or working out of that story. No doubt it might have been better told. But I wish I was five-and-twenty years younger, sitting once more in that dingy little office where we wrangled over this headstrong hero of ours, and had to suppress so many—oh! so very many—of the rows and troubles and fights into which he fell even after he became respectable. The office was handy for Rule's and oysters. We would adjourn for the "delicious mollusc," and then go back again to the editor's room to resume the wrangle. Here we would be interrupted by Julia, who brought the bookbinder's account; or by the interesting but thirsty hack, who brought his copy, and with it an aroma of rum; or by the airy gentleman who wanted to catch science on the Wing, sir—on the Wing; or by the Economic man; or by the irresponsible man, ready for anything. In the evening we would dine together, or go to a theatre, or sit in my chambers and play cards before resuming the wrangle—we used to take an hour of Vingt-un, by way of relaxation. And always during that period, whatever we did, wherever we went, Dick Mortiboy sat between us. Dear old Dick grew quiet towards the end. The wrangling was finished. The inevitable was before him; he must pay for the past. Love could not be his, nor honour, such as comes to most men, nor the quiet *vie de famille*, which is all that life really has to give worth having. His cousin Frank might have love and honour. For him—Dick's brave eyes looked straight before—he had no illusions; for him, the end that belongs to the nineteenth-century ruffler, the man of the West, the sportsman and the gambler, the only end—the bullet from the revolver of his accomplice, was certain and inevitable. So it ended. Dick died. The novel was finished.

Dick died; our friend died; he had his faults—but he was Dick; and he died. And alas! his history was all told and done with; the manuscript finished; the last wrangle over; the fatal word, the melancholy word, *Finis*, written below the last line.

"The Family Scapegrace"

By James Payn

I had written a great many short stories and articles in all sorts of publications, from *Eliza Cook's Journal* to the *Westminster Review*, before I ventured upon writing a novel; and the appearance of them I have since had cause to regret. Not at all because they were "immature," and still less because I am ashamed of them—on the contrary, I still think them rather good—but because the majority of them were not made the most of from a literary point of view, and also went very cheap. As a friend observed to me, who was much my senior, and whose advice was therefore treated with contempt, "You are like an extravagant cook, who wastes too much material on a single dish." The *entrées* of the story-teller—his early and tentative essays in Fiction—if he has really any turn for his calling, are generally open to this criticism. Later on, he becomes more economical (sometimes, indeed, a good deal too much so, because, alas! there is so little in the cupboard), and has a much finer sense of proportion.

I don't know how many years I went on writing narratives of school and college life, and spinning short stories, like a literary spider, out of my own interior, but I don't remember that it was ever borne in upon me that the reservoir could hardly hold out forever, and that it was time to be doing something on a more permanent and extended scale. The cause of that act of prudence and sagacity was owing mainly to a travelling menagerie. I had had in my mind, for sometime, to write a sort of autobiography (of which character first novels almost always consist, or at least partake), but had in truth abstained from doing so on the not unreasonable ground that my life had been wholly destitute of incidents of public interest. True, I had mended that matter by the wholly gratuitous invention of a cheerless home and a wicked sister, but I had hitherto found nothing more attractive to descant upon than my own domestic wrongs. Even if they had existed, it was doubtful whether they would have aroused public indignation, and I mistrusted my powers of making them exist. What I wanted was a dramatic situation or two (a "plot," the evolution of which by no means comes by nature, though the germ is often an inspiration, was at that time beyond me), and especially the opportunity of observation.

My own slender experiences were used up, and imagination had no material to work upon; one can't blow even glass out of nothing at all. Just in the nick of time arrived in Edinburgh, where I was then editing *Chambers's Journal*, Tickeracandua, "the African Lion Tamer." At that time (though I have seen a great deal of them since) lions were entirely out of my line, and also tamers; but this gentleman was a most attractive specimen of his class. Handsome, frank, and intelligent, he took my fancy from the first, and we became great friends. "His actual height," says my notebook, "could scarcely have been less than six feet two, while it was artificially increased by a circlet of cock's feathers set in a coronet, which the majority of enraptured beholders believed to be of virgin gold. A leopard skin, worn after the fashion of a Scotch plaid, set off a jerkin of green leather, while his legs were encased in huge jack boots." This, of course, was his performing dress, and I used to wonder how the leopards (with whom he had a great deal to do) liked his wearing their relative's cast-off clothing. In the "leopard-hunt" (twice a day) these animals raced over him as he stood erect, and each, as it "took off" from his shoulder, left its mark there with its claws. He was so good as to show me his shoulder, which looked as if he had been profusely vaccinated in the wrong place. A much more dangerous, if less painful, experience was his daily (and nightly) doings with the lions. There were two of them, with a lioness of an uncertain temper, who jumped through hoops at his imperious bidding with many a growl and snarl of remonstrance.

"Are you never afraid?" I once asked him tentatively.

"If I was," he answered, quietly, but not contemptuously, "I might count myself from that moment a dead man. Then, you see, I have my whip." It was a carter's whip, good to keep off a dog, but scarcely a lion. "The handle is loaded," he explained, "and I know exactly where to hit 'em with it, if the worst comes to the worst." If I remember right, it was the tip of the nose.

His conversation was delightful, and he often honoured me with his company at supper, when the toils and perils of the day were o'er. Upon the whole, though I have since known many other eminent persons, he has left a more marked impression on me than any of them, and it is no wonder that in those youthful days he influenced my imagination. His autobiography, without his having the least suspicion of the appropriation, became in fact *my* autobiography, as may be read (if there is anybody who has not enjoyed that treat) in "The Family

Scapegrace." But, as my predecessors in the field of Fiction were wont to exclaim, "I am anticipating."

Another official connected with the menagerie gave daily lectures upon the animals, so curiously dry and grave that they filled me with admiration; he was like an embodiment of the answers to "Mangnall's Questions." Whatever suspicions Tickeracandua may have subsequently entertained of me, I am quite sure that "Mr. Mopes" would no more have seen himself in the portrait I drew of him than would the animals under his charge, if their attention had been drawn to them, have recognised their counterfeit presentments outside the show. I also became acquainted with the Earthman and Earthwoman, the slaughterman of the establishment, Mr. and Mrs. Tredgold (its proprietors), and other individuals seldom met with in ordinary society.

The adventures of "Richard Arbour" were, therefore, cut out for me in a most convenient and unexpected fashion, but I had the intelligence to perceive that though the interest they might excite would be dramatic enough, they would be in danger of dealing too much with the animal world to interest adult readers; nor would the narrative have made an attractive book for boys, since I felt it would be too full of fun (for my spirits were very high in those days) to suit juvenile tastes. I knew little of the world, but had seen much of boys (though I had never belonged to the species), and was well aware that, except as regards practical jokes, the boy is not gifted with humour. I accordingly looked about me for some dramatic material of a wholly different kind, and eventually found it in the person of Count Gotsuchakoff.

It was a mistake to call such a sombre and serious individual by so ludicrous a name, but it was a characteristic one. My disposition was at that time lively (not to say frivolous), and the atmosphere I usually lived in was one of mirth, but, as often happens, it had another side to it, which was melancholy almost to melodrama. In after years I found this to be the case in an infinitely greater story-teller, who, while he delighted all the world with humour and pathos, in reality nourished a taste for the weird and terrible, which, though its ghastly face but very rarely showed itself in his writings, was the favourite topic of his familiar and confidential talk. Tickeracandua himself was not dearer to me than the Count, who was almost entirely the offspring of my own invention; and though I have since seen in Nihilist novels a good many gentlemen of the same type, I venture to think that, slightly as he is sketched, he will bear comparison with the best of them. The conception of his long years of enforced silence, and even of the terrible moment in which he forgot that he was dumb, owed its origin, if I remember right, to a child's game that was popular in our nursery. It consisted in resisting the temptation to laugh, and the resolution to reply in tones of gravity when such questions as "Have you heard the Emperor of Morocco is dead?" were put. The adaptation of it, in the substitution of speech for laughter, suddenly suggested itself, like any other happy thought.

Instead of writing straight ahead, as the fancy prompted, which, in my less ambitious attempts at Fiction (like all young writers) I had hitherto done, I had all these materials pretty well arranged in my mind before sitting down to write my first book. It was, after all, only a string of adventures, but it is still, and I think deservedly, a popular book. The question with its author, however, was how, when it was finished, he was to get it published. I took it to my friend, Robert Chambers, and asked for his opinion about it. He looked at the manuscript, which was certainly not in such good handwriting as his own, and observed slyly—

"Would you mind just reading a bit of it?"

I had never done such a thing before, nor have I since, and the proposal was a little staggering, not to my *amour propre*, but to my natural modesty. Moreover, I mistrusted my ability to do justice to it, remembering what the poet has said about reading one's own productions:

> The chariot wheels jar in the gates through which we drive them forth.

However, I started with it, and notwithstanding that we were subjected to "jars" (one by the servant, who came to put coals on the fire, just at a crisis, and made me at heart a murderer), the specimen was pronounced satisfactory.

"I think it will suit nicely for the *Journal*," said my friend, which I think were the pleasantest words I ever heard from the mouth of man. I might have taken them, indeed, as a good omen; for though I have since written more novels than I can count, I have never failed to secure serial publication for everyone of them. "This gentleman's novels are suitable enough for serial publication," once wrote a critic of them, intending to be very particularly disagreeable, but it aroused no emotion in my breast warmer than gratitude.

So "The Family Scapegrace" came out in *Chambers's Journal*. I do not remember whether it had any effect upon its circulation, but it was well spoken of, and there was at least one person in the world who thought it a masterpiece. The difficulty, which no one but a young and unknown writer can estimate, was to get a publisher to share in this belief. For many years afterwards I published my books anonymously (*i.e.*, "by the author" of so and so), and many a humorous interview I had with various denizens of Paternoster Row, to whom I (very strongly) recommended them, by proxy. "If I were speaking to the author," they said, "it would be unpleasant to say this (that, and the other of a deprecatory character), but with *you* we can be quite frank." And they were sometimes very frank; and, though I didn't much like it at the time, their candour (when I had sold the book tolerably well) tickled me afterwards immensely. For persons who have enjoyed this experience, mere literary criticism has henceforth no terrors.

"The Family Scapegrace," however, had appeared under my own name, so that concealment was out of the question; it was in one volume, a form of publication which, at that time at all events (though I see they now affirm the contrary), was unpopular with the libraries, and I was quite an unknown novelist. Under these circumstances, I have never forgotten the kindness of Mr. Douglas (of the firm of Edmonston & Douglas), who gave me fifty pounds for the first edition of the book—by which enterprise he lost his money. There were many reasons for it, no doubt, though the story has since done well enough, but I think the chief of them was the alteration of the title to "Richard Arbour," which, contrary to the wishes both of myself and my publisher, was insisted upon by a leading librarian. It is difficult, nowadays, to guess his reason, but people were more "square-toed" in those times, and I fancy he thought his highly respectable customers would scent something Bohemian, if not absolutely scampish, in a Scapegrace. A mere name is not an attractive title for a book; though many books so called—such as "Martin Chuzzlewit" and "Robinson Crusoe"—have become immensely popular, they owed nothing to their baptism; and certainly "Richard Arbour" prospered better when he got rid of his rather commonplace name.

A rather curious incident took place with respect to this book, which annoyed me greatly at the time, because I was quite unacquainted with the queer crotchets and imaginary grievances that would-be literary persons often take into their heads. Somebody wrote to complain that he had written (not published) a story upon the same lines, and even incidents, as "The Family Scapegrace," just before its appearance in the columns of *Chambers's Journal*, and the delicate inference he drew was that, whether in my capacity of editor or otherwise, I must have somehow got hold of it. He gave the exact date of the conclusion of his own composition, which was prior to the commencement of my story in the *Journal*.

Conscious of innocence, but troubled by so disagreeable an imputation, I laid the matter before Robert Chambers.

"You are not so versed in the ways of this class of person as I am," he said, smiling; "but since he has been so injudicious as to give a date, I think we can put him out of court. I am one of those methodical individuals who keep a diary." And on reference to it, he found that I had read him my story long before that of my traducer, according to his own account, had left his hands.

It was a small matter, but proved a useful lesson to me, for there is a great deal of imposture of this kind going on in the literary world; sometimes, as perhaps in this case, the result of mere egotistic fancy, but also sometimes begotten by the desire to levy blackmail.

The above, so far as I can remember them, are the circumstances under which I published my first novel. I am sorry to add that poor Tickeracandua, to whom it owed so much, subsequently met the very fate in reality which I had assigned to him in fiction; though as good a fellow as many I have met *out* of a show, he came to the same end as "Don't Care" did in the nursery story, and was "eaten (or at all events killed) by lions."

"The Wreck of the 'Grosvenor'"

By W. Clark Russell

I am complimented by an invitation to tell what I can recollect of the writing, publication, and reception of the earliest of my sea books, "The Wreck of the 'Grosvenor.'" I approach the subject with diffidence, and ask the reader to forgive me if he thinks or finds me unduly egotistical. "John Holdsworth: Chief Mate," preceded "The Wreck of the 'Grosvenor.'" I do not regard that story as a novel of the sea. I was reluctant and timid in dealing with ocean topics when the scheme of that tale came into my head; I contented myself with pulling off my shoes and socks and walking about ankle deep into the ripples. But in the "Grosvenor" I went to sea like a man; I signed articles aboard her as second mate; I had ruffians for shipmates, and the stench of the harness-cask was the animating influence of the narrative. It is the first sea book I ever wrote, in the sense, I mean, that its successors are sea books: what I have to say, therefore, agreeably to the plan of these personal contributions, will refer to it.

And first, I must write a few words about my own experience as a sailor. I went to sea in the year 1858, when I was a child of thirteen years and a few months old. My first ship was a well-known Australian liner, the "Duncan Dunbar," commanded by an old salt, named Neatby, who will always be memorable to me for his habit of wearing the tall chimney-pot hat of the London streets in all weathers and parallels, whether in the roasting calms of the Equator, or in the snow-darkened hurricanes of the Horn. I went to sea as a "midshipman" as it is termed, though I never could persuade myself that a lad in the Merchant Service, no matter how heavy might be the premium his friends paid for him, has a right to a title of grade or rating that belongs essentially and peculiarly to the Royal Navy. I signed for a shilling a month, and with the rest of us (there were ten) was called "young gentleman"; but we were put to work which an able seaman would have been within his rights in refusing, as being what is called "boys'" duty. I need not be particular. Enough that the discipline was as rough as though we had been lads in the forecastle, with a huge boatswain and brutal boatswain's mates to look after us. We paid ten guineas each as a contribution to some imagination of a stock of eatables for the midshipmen's berth; but my memory carries no more than a few tins of preserved potatoes, a great number of bottles of pickles, and a cask of exceedingly moist sugar. Therefore, we were thrown upon the ship's provisions, and I very soon became intimately acquainted with the quality and nature of the stores served out to forecastle hands.

I made, but not after the manner of Gulliver, several voyages into remote nations of the world, and in the eight years I was at sea I picked up enough knowledge to qualify me to give the public a few new ideas about the ocean life. Yet when the scribbling mania possessed me it was long before I could summon courage to write about the sea and sailors. I asked myself, Who is interested in the Merchant Service? What public shall I find to listen to me? Those who read novels want stories about love and elopements, abductions, and the several violations of the sanctities of domestic life. The great mass of readers—those who support the circulating libraries—are ladies. Will it be possible to interest ladies in forecastle life and in the prosaics of the cabin?

Then, again, I was frightened by the Writer for Boys. *He* was very much at sea. I never picked up a book of his without lighting upon some hideous act of piracy, some astounding and unparalleled shipwreck, some marvellous island of treasure. This writer, of a clan numerous as Wordsworth's "little lot of stars," warned me off and affrighted me. His paper ship had so long and successfully filled the public eye that I shrank from launching anything real, anything with strakes and treenails, anything with running rigging so leading that a sailor would exactly know what to let go when the order was given. In plain English, I judged that the sea story had been irremediably depressed, and rendered wholly ridiculous by the strenuous periodic and Christmas labours of the Writer for Boys. Had he not sunk even Marryat and Michael Scott, who, because they wrote about the sea, were compelled in due course by the publishers to address themselves exclusively to boys! The late George Cupples—a man of fine genius—in the course of a letter to me, complained warmly of being made to figure as "Captain" George Cupples upon the title-page of his admirable work, "The Green Hand." He assured me that he was no captain, and that his name thus written was merely a bookseller's dodge to recommend his story to boys.

And, still, I would sometimes think that if I would but take heart and go afloat in imagination, under the old red flag, I should find within the circle of the horizon such materials for a book as might recommend it, at all events on the score of freshness. Only two writers had dealt with the mercantile side of the ocean life—Dana, the author of "Two Years before the Mast," and Herman Melville, both of them, it is needless to say, Americans. I could not recollect a book, written by an Englishman, relating, as a work of fiction, to shipboard life on the high seas under the flag of the Merchant Service. I excluded the Writer for Boys. I could recall no author who, himself a practical seaman, one who had slept with sailors, eaten with them, gone aloft with them, and suffered with them, had produced a book, a novel—call it what you will—wholly based on what I may term the inner life of the forecastle and the cabin.

It chanced one day that a big ship, with a mastheaded colour, telling of trouble on board, let go her anchor in the Downs. I then lived in a town which overlooks those waters. The crew of the ship had mutinied: they had carried the vessel halfway down Channel, when, discovering by that time what sort of provisions had been shipped for them, they forced the master to shift his helm for the inwards course. The crew of thirteen or fourteen hairy, queerly attired fellows, in Scotch caps, divers-coloured shirts, dungaree breeches stuffed into half wellingtons, were brought before the magistrates. The bench consisted of an old sea captain, who had lost a ship in his day through the ill conduct of his crew, and whose hatred of the forecastle hand was strong and peculiar; a parson, who knew about as much of the sea as his wife; a medical practitioner, and a schoolmaster. I was present, and listened to the men's evidence, and I also heard the captain's story. Samples of the food were produced. A person with whom I had some acquaintance found me an opportunity to examine and taste samples of the forecastle provisions of the ship whose crew had mutinied. Nothing more atrociously nasty could be found amongst the neglected putrid sweepings of a butcher's back premises. Nothing viler in the shape of food ever set a famished mongrel hiccoughing. Nevertheless, this crew of thirteen or fourteen men, for refusing to sail in the vessel unless fresh forecastle stores were shipped, were sent to gaol for terms ranging from three to six weeks.

Sometime earlier than this there had been legislation helpful to the seaman through the humane and impassioned struggles of Mr. Samuel Plimsoll. The crazy, rotten old coaster had been knocked into staves. The avaricious owner had been compelled to load with some regard to the safety of sailors. But I could not help thinking that the shore-going menace of the sailor's life did not lie merely in overloaded ships, and in crazy, porous hulls. Mutinies were incessantly happening in consequence of the loathsome food shipped for sailors' use, and many disasters attended these outbreaks. When I came away from the magistrates' court, after hearing the men sentenced, I found my mind full of that crew's grievance. I reflected upon what Mr. Plimsoll had done, and how much of the hidden parts of the sea life remained to be exposed to the public eye, to the advantage of the sailor, providing the subject should be dealt with by one who had himself suffered, and very well understood what he sat down to write about. This put into my head the idea of the tale which I afterwards called "The Wreck of the 'Grosvenor.'" I said to myself, I'll found a story on a mutiny at sea, occasioned entirely by the shipment of bad provisions for the crew. No writer has as yet touched this ugly feature of the life. Dana is silent. Herman Melville merely drops a joke or two as he rolls out of the caboose with a cube of salt horse in his hand. It has never been made a serious canvas of. And yet deeper tragedies lie in the stinking harness-cask than in the started butt. There are wilder and bloodier possibilities in a barrel of rotten pork, and in a cask of worm-riddled ship's bread, than in a whole passage of shifting cargoes, and in a long round voyage of deadweight that sinks to the wash-streak.

But if I was to find a public I must make my book a romance. I must import the machinery of the petticoat. The pannikin of rum I proposed to offer must be palatable enough to tempt the lips of the ladies to sip it. My publisher would want a market, and if Messrs. Mudie and Smith would have none of me I should write in vain; for assuredly I was not going to find a public among sailors. Sailors don't read: a good many of them *can't* read. Those who can have little leisure, and they do not care to fill up their spare hours with yarns of a calling which eighty out of every hundred of them loathe. So I schemed out a nautical romance and went to work, and in two months and a week I finished the story of "The Wreck of the 'Grosvenor.'"

Whilst I was writing it an eminent publisher, a gentleman whose friendship I had been happy in possessing for many years, asked me to let him have a sea story. I think he had been looking into "John Houldsworth: Chief Mate," which some months before this time had been received with much kindness by the reviewers. I sent him the manuscript of "The Wreck of the 'Grosvenor.'" One of his readers was a lady, and to this lady my friend the publisher forwarded the manuscript, with a request for a report on its merits. Now to send the manuscript of a sea book to a woman! To submit a narrative abounding in marine terms, thunder-charged with the bully-in-our-alley passions of the forecastle, throbbing with suppressed oaths, clamorous with rolling oceans, the like of which no female would ever dream of leaving her bunk to behold—to submit all this, and how much more, to a lady for an opinion on its merits! Of course, the poor woman barely understood a third of what she looked at, and as, obviously she couldn't quite collect the meaning of the remainder, she pronounced against the whole. She called it a "catalogue of ship's furniture," and the manuscript came back to me. I never regret this. I do not believe that this sea book would have cut a figure in my old esteemed friend's list. Publishers are well known by the public for the sort of intellectual fare they deal in. If I desired a charming story about flirtation, divorce, inconvenient husbands, the state of the soul when it has flown out of the body, the passions of the female heart whilst it still beats hot in the breast, I should turn to my friend's list, well assured of handsome satisfaction. But I don't think I could read a sea book published by him. I should suspect the marine qualities of a Jack who had run foul of, and got smothered up in, a whole wardrobe of female apparel, grinning with a scarcely sunburnt face through the horse-collar of a crinoline, the deep sea roll of his gait hampered and destroyed by the clinging folds of a flannel petticoat.

Be this as it may, I sent the manuscript of "The Wreck of the 'Grosvenor'" to my old friend Edward Marston, of the firm of Sampson Low & Co. The firm offered me fifty pounds for it; I took the money and signed the agreement, in which I disposed of all rights. Do I murmur over the recollection of this fifty pounds which, with another ten pounds kindly sent to me by Mr. Marston as the whole of, or a part of, a cheque received from Messrs. Harper & Brothers, was all I ever got for this sea book? Certainly not. The transaction was absolutely fair, and what leaning there was was in my favour. The book was an experiment; it was published anonymously; it might have fallen dead. Happily for publisher and author, the book made its way. I believe it was immediately successful in America, and that its reception there somewhat influenced inquiry here. American critics who try to vex me say that my books never would have been read in this country but for what was said of them in the States, and for the publicity provided for them there by the twenty-cent editions. How far this is true I don't know; but certainly the Yankees are handsomer and prompter in their recognition of what pleases them than we are on our side. What they like they raise a great cry over, and the note of so mighty a concourse, I don't doubt, fetches an echo out of distances below the horizon.

It is many years now since "The Wreck of the 'Grosvenor'" was written, and I do not very clearly recollect its reception in this country. I believe it speedily went into a second edition. But before we talk of an edition seriously we must first learn the number of copies which make it. Since this was written, my friend, Mr. R. B. Marston, of the firm of Sampson Low & Co., has been good enough to look into the sales of "The Wreck of the 'Grosvenor,'" and he informs me that down to 1891 there had been sold 34,950 copies. One of the most cordial welcomes the story received was from *Vanity Fair*. I supposed that the review was written by the editor, Mr. Thomas Gibson Bowles, until I learnt that the late Mr. James Runciman was the author. The critics on the whole were generous. They thought the book fresh. They judged that it was an original piece of work wrought largely out of the personal experiences of the writer. One gentleman, indeed, said that he had crossed the Channel on several occasions between Boulogne and Folkestone, but had never witnessed such seas as I described; and another that he had frequently travelled to Plymouth on the Great Western Railway in company with sailors, but had never met such seamen as the forecastle hands I depicted. The book is considered my best—this, perhaps, because it was my first, and its reputation lies in the memory and impression of its freshness. It is far from being my best. Were it my property I would re-write it. I had quitted the sea some years when I wrote the story, and here and there my memory played me false; that is to say, in the direction of certain minute technicalities and in accounts of the internal discipline of the ship. Yet, on the whole, the blunders are few considering how very complicated a fabric a vessel is, and how ceaselessly one needs to go on living the life of the sea to hold all parts of it clear to the sight of the mind. Professionally, the influence of the book has been small. I have heard that it made one ship-owner sorry and rather virtuous, and that for sometime his harness-casks went their voyages fairly sweet. He is, however, but a solitary figure, the lonesome Crusoe of my little principality of fancy. As a piece of literature, "The Wreck of the 'Grosvenor'" has been occasionally imitated. Mr. Plimsoll, I understand, has lately been dealing with the subject of sailors' food. I heartily wish success to his efforts.

"Physiological Æsthetics" and "Philistia"

By Grant Allen

The story of my first book is a good deal mixed, and, like many other stories, cannot be fully understood without some previous allusion to what historians call "the causes which led to it." For my first book was not my first novel, and it is the latter, I take it, not the former, that an expectant world, as represented by the readers of this volume, is anxious to hear about. I first blossomed into print with "Physiological Æsthetics" in 1877—the title alone will be enough for most people—and it was not till seven years later that I wrote and published my earliest long work of fiction, which I called "Philistia." I wasn't born a novelist, I was only made one. Philosophy and science were the first loves of my youth. I dropped into romance as many men drop into drink, or opium-eating, or other bad practices, not of native perversity, but by pure force of circumstances. And this is how fate (or an enterprising publisher) turned me from an innocent and impecunious naturalist into a devotee of the muse of shilling shockers.

When I left Oxford in 1870, with a decent degree and nothing much else in particular to brag about, I took perforce to that refuge of the destitute, the trade of schoolmaster. To teach Latin and Greek verse at Brighton College, Cheltenham College, Reading Grammar School, successively, was the extremely uncongenial task imposed upon me by the chances of the universe. But in 1873, Providence, disguised as the Colonial Office, sent me out in charge of a new Government College at Spanish Town, Jamaica. I had always been psychological, and in the space and leisure of the lazy Tropics I began to excogitate by slow degrees various expansive works on the science of mind, the greater number of which still remain unwritten. Returning to England in '76 I found myself out of work, and so committed to paper some of my views on the origin of the higher pleasure we derive from natural or artistic products; and I called my book "Physiological Æsthetics." It was not my very first attempt at literature; already I had produced about a hundred or more magazine articles on various philosophical and scientific subjects, everyone of which I sent to the editors of leading reviews, and everyone of which was punctually "Declined with thanks," or committed without even that polite formality to the editorial waste paper basket. Nothing daunted by failure, however, I wrote on and on, and made up my mind, in my interval of forced idleness, to print a book of my own at all hazards.

I wrote "Physiological Æsthetics" in lodgings at Oxford. When it was finished and carefully revised, I offered it to Messrs. Henry S. King & Co., who were then leading publishers of philosophical literature. Mr. Kegan Paul, their reader, reported doubtfully of the work. It was not likely to pay, he said, but it contained good matter, and the firm would print it for me on the usual commission. I was by no means rich—for fear of exaggeration I am stating the case mildly—but I believed somehow in "Physiological Æsthetics." I was young then, and I hope the court of public opinion will extend to me, on that ground, the indulgence usually shown to juvenile offenders. But I happened to possess a little money just at that moment, granted me as compensation for the abolition of my office in Jamaica. Messrs. King reported that the cost of production (that mysterious entity so obnoxious to the soul of the Society of Authors) would amount to about a hundred guineas. A hundred guineas was a lot of money then; but, being young, I risked it. It was better than if I had taken it to Monte Carlo, anyway. So I wrote to Mr. Paul with heedless haste to publish away right off, and he published away right off accordingly. When the bill came in, it was, if I recollect aright, somewhere about 120*l.* I paid it without a murmur; I got my money's worth. The book appeared in a stately green cover, with my name in front, and looked very philosophical, and learned, and psychological.

Poor "Physiological Æsthetics" had a very hard fate. When I come to look back upon the circumstances calmly and dispassionately now, I'm not entirely surprised at its unhappy end. It was a good book in its way, to be sure, though it's me that says it as oughtn't to say it, and it pleased the few who cared to read it; but it wasn't the sort of literature the public wanted. The public, you know, doesn't hanker after philosophy. Darwin, and Herbert Spencer, and the Editor of *Mind*, and people of that sort, tried my work and liked it; in point of fact, my poor little venture gained me at once, an unknown man, the friendship of not a few whose friendship was worth having. But financially, "Physiological Æsthetics" was a dead failure; it wasn't the sort of work to sell briskly at the bookstalls. Mr. Smith would have none of it. The reviews, indeed, were, almost without exception, favourable; the volume went off well for a treatise of its kind—that is to say, we got rid of nearly 300 copies;

but even so, it left a deficit of some forty or fifty pounds to the bad against me. Finally, the remaining stock fell a victim to the flames in Mr. Kegan Paul's historical fire, when many another stout volume perished: and that was the end of my *magnum opus*. Peace to its ashes! Mr. Paul gave me 15*l.* as compensation for loss sustained, and I believe I came out some 30*l.* a loser by this, my first serious literary venture. In all these matters, however, I speak from memory alone, and it is possible I may be slightly wrong in my figures.

But though "Physiological Æsthetics" was a financial failure, it paid me in the end, both scientifically and commercially. Not only did it bring me into immediate contact with several among the leaders of thought in London, but it also made my name known in a very modest way, and induced editors—those arbiters of literary fate—to give a second glance at my unfortunate manuscripts. Almost immediately after its appearance, Leslie Stephen (I omit the Mr., *honoris causa*) accepted two papers of mine for publication in the *Cornhill*. "Carving a Cocoanut" was the first, and it brought me in twelve guineas. That was the very first money I earned in literature. I had been out of work for months, the abolition of my post in Jamaica having thrown me on my beam-ends, and I was overjoyed at so much wealth poured suddenly in upon me. Other magazine articles followed in due course, and before long I was earning a modest—a very modest—and precarious income, yet enough to support myself and my family. Moreover, Sir William Hunter, who was then engaged on his gigantic "Gazetteer of India," gave me steady employment in his office at Edinburgh, and I wrote with my own hand the greater part of the articles on the North-West Provinces, the Punjaub, and Sind, in those twelve big volumes.

Meanwhile, I was hard at work in my leisure moments (for I have sometimes some moments which I regard as leisure) on another ambitious scientific work, which I called "The Colour-Sense." This book I published on the half-profits system with Trübner. Compared with my first unhappy venture, "The Colour-Sense" might be counted a distinct success. It brought me in, during the course of about ten years, something like 25*l.* or 30*l.* As it only took me eighteen months to write, and involved little more than five or six thousand references, this result may be regarded as very fair pay for an educated man's time and labour. I have sometimes been reproached by thoughtless critics for deserting the noble pursuit of science in favour of fiction and filthy lucre. If those critics think twenty pounds a year a sufficient income for a scientific writer to support himself and a growing family upon—well, they are perfectly at liberty to devote their own pens to the instruction of their kind without the slightest remonstrance or interference on my part.

I won't detail in full the history of my various intermediate books, most of which were published first as newspaper articles, and afterwards collected and put forth on a small royalty. Time is short, and art is long, so I'll get on at once to my first novel. I drifted into fiction by the sheerest accident. My friend, Mr. Chatto, most generous of men, was one of my earliest and staunchest literary supporters. From the outset of my journalistic days, he printed my articles in *Belgravia* and the *Gentleman's Magazine* with touching fidelity; and I take this opportunity of saying in public that to his kindness and sympathy I owe as much as to anyone in England. Some people will have it there is no such thing as "generosity" in publishers. I beg leave to differ from them. I know the commercial value of literary work as well as any man, and I venture to say that both from Mr. Chatto and from Mr. Arrowsmith, of Bristol, I have met, time and again, with what I cannot help describing as most generous treatment. One day it happened that I wanted to write a scientific article on the impossibility of knowing one had seen a ghost, even if one saw one. For convenience sake, and to make the moral clearer, I threw the argument into narrative form, but without the slightest intention of writing a story. It was published in *Belgravia* under the title of "Our Scientific Observations on a Ghost," and was reprinted later in my little volume of "Strange Stories." A little while after, to my immense surprise, Mr. Chatto wrote to ask me whether I could supply him with another story, like the last I had written, for the *Belgravia Annual*. I was rather taken aback at this singular request, as I hadn't the slightest idea I could do anything at all in the way of fiction. Still, like a good journalist, I never refuse an order of any sort; so I sat down at once and wrote a tale about a mummy on the ghastliest and most approved Christmas number pattern. Strange to say, Mr. Chatto again printed it, and, what was still more remarkable, asked for more of the same description. From that time forth, I went on producing short stories for *Belgravia*; but I hardly took them seriously, being immersed at the time in biological study. I looked upon my own pretensions in the way of fiction as an amiable fad of my kind friend Chatto; and not to prejudice any little scientific reputation I might happen to have earned, I published them all under the carefully veiled pseudonym of "J. Arbuthnot Wilson."

I would probably never have gone any further on my downward path had it not been for the accidental intervention of another believer in my powers as a story-writer. I had sent to *Belgravia* a little tale about a Chinaman, entitled "Mr. Chung," and written perhaps rather more seriously and carefully than my previous efforts. This happened to attract the attention of Mr. James Payn, who had then just succeeded to the editorship of the *Cornhill*. I had been a constant contributor to the *Cornhill* under Leslie Stephen's management, and by a singular coincidence I received almost at the same time two letters from Mr. Payn, one of them addressed to me in my own name, and regretting that he would probably be unable to insert my scientific papers in his magazine in future; the other, sent through Chatto & Windus to the imaginary J. Arbuthnot Wilson, and asking for a short story somewhat in the style of my "admirable Mr. Chung."

Encouraged by the discovery that so good a judge of fiction thought well of my humble efforts at story-writing, I sat down at once and produced two pieces for the *Cornhill*. One was "The Reverend John Creedy"—a tale of a black parson who reverted to savagery—which has perhaps attracted more attention than any other of my short stories. The other, which I myself immensely prefer, was "The Curate of Churnside." Both were so well noticed that I began to think seriously of fiction as an alternative subject. In the course of the next year I wrote several more sketches of the same sort, which were published, either anonymously or still under the pseudonym, in the *Cornhill*, *Longmans'*, *The Gentleman's*, and *Belgravia*. If I recollect aright, the first suggestion to collect and reprint them all in a single volume came from Mr. Chatto. They were published as "Strange Stories," under my own name, and I thus, for the first time, acknowledged my desertion of my earliest loves—science and philosophy—for the less profound but more lucrative pursuit of literature.

"Strange Stories" was well received and well reviewed. Its reception gave me confidence for future ventures. Acting upon James Payn's advice, I set to work seriously upon a three-volume novel. My first idea was to call it "Born out of Due Time," as it narrated the struggles of a Socialist thinker a century in front of his generation; but, at Mr. Chatto's suggestion, the title was afterwards changed to "Philistia." I desired, if possible, to run it through the *Cornhill*, and Mr. Payn promised to take it into his most favourable consideration for that purpose. However, when the unfinished manuscript was submitted in due time to his editorial eye, he rightly objected that it was far too socialistic for the tastes of his public. He said it would rather repel than attract readers. I was disappointed at the time. I see now that, as an editor, he was perfectly right; I was giving the public what I felt and thought and believed myself, not what the public felt and thought and wanted. The education of an English novelist consists entirely in learning to subordinate all his own ideas and tastes and opinions to the wishes and beliefs of the inexorable British matron.

Mr. Chatto, however, was prepared to accept the undoubted risk of publishing "Philistia." Only, to meet his views, the *dénoûment* was altered. In the original version, the hero came to a bad end, as a hero in real life who is in advance of his age, and consistent and honest, must always do. But the British matron, it seems, likes her novels to "end well"; so I married him off instead, and made him live happily ever afterward. Mr. Chatto gave me a lump sum down for serial rights and copyright, and ran "Philistia" through the pages of *The Gentleman's*. When it finally appeared in book form, it obtained on the whole more praise than blame, and, as it paid a great deal better than scientific journalism, it decided me that my *rôle* in life henceforth must be that of a novelist. And a novelist I now am, good, bad, or indifferent.

If anybody gathers, however, from this simple narrative, that my upward path from obscurity to a very modest modicum of popularity and success was a smooth and easy one, he is immensely mistaken. I had a ten years' hard struggle for bread, into the details of which I don't care to enter. It left me broken in health and spirit, with all the vitality and vivacity crushed out of me. I suppose the object of this series of papers is to warn off ingenuous and aspiring youth from the hardest worked and worst paid of the professions. If so, I would say earnestly to the ingenuous and aspiring—"Brain for brain, in no market can you sell your abilities to such poor advantage. Don't take to literature if you've capital enough in hand to buy a good broom, and energy enough to annex a vacant crossing."

"The Shadow of a Crime"

By Hall Caine

I cannot follow Mr. Besant with any pitiful story of rejection at the hands of publishers. If refusal is quite the best thing that can happen to the candidate for literary honours, my fate has not been favourable. No tale of mine has yet passed from publishing house to publishing house. Except the first of the series, my stories have been accepted before they have been read. In two or three instances they have been bought before they have been written. It has occurred to me, as to others, to have two or three publishers offering terms for the same book. I have even been offered half payment in hand on account of a book which I could not hope to write for years, and might never write at all. Thus the most helpful confession which the more or less successful man of letters can make for the comfort and cheer of his younger and less fortunate brethren, it is out of my power to offer.

But I reflect that this is true of my literary experiences in the character of a novelist only. I had an earlier and semi-subterranean career that was very different. At eighteen I wrote a poem of a mystical sort, which was printed (not at my own risk) and published under a pseudonym. Happily, no man will ever identify me behind the romantic name wherein I hid my own. Only one literary man knew my secret. That was George Gilfillan, and he is dead. Then at twenty I wrote an autobiography for another person, and was paid ten pounds for it. These were really my first books, and I grow quite hot when I think of them. At five-and-twenty I came up to London with the manuscript of a critical work, which I had written while at Liverpool. Somebody had recommended that I should submit it to a certain great publishing house, and I took it in person. At the door of the office I was told to write my own name, and the name of the person whom I wished to see, and to state the nature of my business. I did so, and the boy who took my message brought back word that I might leave my manuscript for consideration. It seemed to me that somebody might have seen me for a minute, but I had expected too much. The manuscript was carefully tied up in brown paper, and so I left it.

After waiting three torturing weeks for the decision of the publishers, I made bold to call again. At the same little box at the door of the office

I had once more to fill up the same little document. The boy took it in, and I was left to sit on his table, to look at the desk which he had been whittling away with his penknife, to wait and to tremble. After a time I heard a footstep returning. I thought it might be the publisher or the editor of the house. It was the boy back again. He had a pile of loose sheets of white paper in his hands. They were the sheets of my book. "The editor's compliments, sir, and—thank you," said the boy, and my manuscript went sprawling over the table. I gathered it up, tucked it as deep as possible into the darkness, under the wings of my Inverness cape, and went downstairs ashamed, humiliated, crushed, and broken-spirited. Not quite that, either, for I remember that, as I got to the fresh air at the door, my gorge rose within me, and I cried in my heart, "By God! you shall—" and something proud and vain.

I dare say it was all right and proper and in good order. The book was afterwards published, and I think it sold well. I hardly know whether I ought to say that the editor should have shown me more courtesy. It was all a part of the anarchy of things which Mr. Hardy considers the rule of life. But the sequel is worth telling. That editor became my personal friend. He is dead, and he was a good and able man. Of course he remembered nothing of this incident, and I never poisoned one hour of our intercourse by telling him how, when I was young and a word of cheer would have buoyed me up, he made me drink the waters of Marah. And three times since that day the publishing house I speak of has come to me with the request that I should write a book for them. I have never been able to do so, but I have outgrown my bitterness, and, of course, I show no malice. Indeed, I have now the best reasons for wishing the great enterprise well. But if literary confessions are worth anything, this one may perhaps be a seed that will somewhere find grateful soil. Keep a good heart, even if you have to knock in vain at many doors, and kick about the backstairs of the house of letters. There is room enough inside.

I wrote and edited sundry things during my first years in London, but not until I had published a story did I feel that I had so much as touched the consciousness of the public.

Hence, my first novel may very properly be regarded as my first book, and if I have no tale to tell of heart-broken impediments in getting it published, I have something to say of the difficulty of getting it written. The novel is called "The Shadow of a Crime," but title it had none until it was finished, and a friend christened it. I cannot remember when the story was begun, because I cannot recall a time when the idea of it did not exist in my mind. Something of the same kind is true of every tale I have ever written or shall ever write. I think it must be in the nature of imagination that an imaginative idea does not spring into being, that it has no spontaneous generation, but, as a germinating conception, a shadow of a vision, always comes floating from somewhere out of the back chambers of memory. You are waiting for the central thought that shall link together incidents that you have gleaned from among the stubble of many fields, for the *motif* that shall put life and meaning into the characters that you have gathered and grouped, and one morning, as you awake, just at that moment when you are between the land of light and the mists of sleep, and as your mind is grappling back for the vanishing form of some delicious dream, a dim but familiar ghost of an idea comes up unbidden for the hundredth time, and you say to yourself, with surprise at your own stupidity, "That's it!"

The idea of my first novel moved about me in this way for many years before I recognised it. As usually happens, it came in the shape of a story. I think it was, in actual fact, first of all, a tale of a grandfather. My mother's father was a Cumberland man, and he was full of the lore of the hills and dales. One of the oldest legends of the Lake mountains tells of the time of the plague. The people were afraid to go to market, afraid to meet at church, and afraid to pass on the highway. When any lonely body was ill, the nearest neighbour left meat and drink at the door of the afflicted house, and knocked and ran away. In these days, a widow with two sons lived in one of the darkest of the valleys. The younger son died, and the body had to be carried over the mountains to be buried. Its course lay across Sty Head Pass, a bleak and "brant" place, where the winds are often high. The eldest son, a strong-hearted lad, undertook the duty. He strapped the coffin on to the back of a young horse, and they started away. The day was wild, and on the top of the pass, where the path dips into Wastdale, between the breast of Great Gable and the heights of Scawfell, the wind rose to a gale. The horse was terrified. It broke away and galloped over the fells, carrying its burden with it. The lad followed and searched for it, but in vain, and he had to go home at last, unsatisfied.

This was in the spring, and nearly all the summer through the surviving son of the widow was out on the mountains, trying to recover the runaway horse, but never once did he catch sight of it, though sometimes, as he turned homeward at night, he thought he heard, in the gathering darkness, above the sough of the wind, the horse's neigh.

Then winter came, and the mother died. Once more the dead body had to be carried over the fells for burial, and once again the coffin was strapped on the back of a horse. It was an old mare that was chosen this time, the mother of the young one that had been lost. The snow lay deep on the pass, and from the cliffs of the Scawfell pikes it hung in great toppling masses. All went well with the little funeral party until they came to the top of the pass, and though the day was dead calm the son held the rein with a hand that was like a vice. But just as the mare reached the spot where the wind had frightened the young horse, there was a terrific noise. An immense body of the snow had parted at that instant from the beetling heights overhead, and rushed down into the valley with the movement as of a mighty earthquake, and the deafening sound as of a peal of thunder. The dale echoed and re-echoed from side to side, and from height to height. The old mare was affrighted; she reared, leapt, flung her master away, and galloped off. When they had recovered from their consternation, the funeral party gave chase, and at length, down in a hollow place, they thought they saw what they were in search of. It was a horse with something strapped on its back. When they came up with it they found it was the *young* horse, with the coffin of the younger son. They led it away and buried the body that it had carried so long, but the old mare they never recovered, and the body of the mother never found sepulchre.

Such was the legend, sufficiently terrible, and even ghastly, which was the germ of my first novel. Its fascination for me lay in its shadow and suggestion of the supernatural. I thought it had all the grip of a ghost story without ever passing out of the world of reality. Imagination played about the position of that elder son, and ingenuity puzzled itself for the sequel to his story. What did he think? What did he feel? What were his superstitions? What became of him? Did he die mad, or was he a MAN, and did he rise out of all doubt and terror? I cannot say how many years this ghost of a conception (with various brothers and sisters of a similar complexion) haunted my mind before I recognised it as the central incident of a story, the faggot for a fire from which other incidents might radiate and imaginary characters take life. When I began to think of it in this practical way I was about six-and-twenty, and was lodging in a lonely farmhouse in the Vale of St. John.

Rossetti was with me, for I had been up to London at his request, and had brought him down to my retreat. The story of that sojourn among the mountains I have told elsewhere. It lives in my memory as a very sweet and sad experience. The poet was a dying man. He spent a few hours of everyday in painful efforts to paint a picture. His nights were long, for sleep never came to him until the small hours of the morning; his sight was troublesome, and he could not read with ease; he was in that condition of ill-health when he could not bear to be alone, and thus he and I were much together. I was just then looking vaguely to the career of a public lecturer, and was delivering a long course of lectures at Liverpool. The subject was prose fiction, and to fortify myself for the work I was reading the masterpieces over again. Seeing this, Rossetti suggested that I should read aloud, and I did so. Many an evening we passed in this way. The farmhouse stood at the foot of a fell by the side of the lowest pool of a ghyll, Fishers' Ghyll, and the roar of falling waters could be heard from within. On the farther side of the vale there were black crags where ravens lived, and in the unseen bed of the dale between lay the dark waters of Thirlmere. The surroundings were striking to the eye and ear in the daylight, but when night came, and the lamp was lit, and the curtains were drawn, and darkness covered everything outside, they were yet more impressive to the imagination. I remember those evenings with gratitude and some pain. The little oblong room, the dull thud of the ghyll like faint thunder overhead, the crackle of the wood fire, myself reading aloud, and Rossetti in a long sack painting coat, his hands thrust into its upright pockets, walking with his heavy and uncertain step to and fro, to and fro, laughing sometimes his big deep laugh, and sometimes sitting down to wipe his moist spectacles and clear his dim eyes. The autumn was far spent, and the nights were long. Not rarely the dead white gleams of the early dawn before the coming of the sun met the yellow light of our candles as we passed on the staircase going to bed a little window that looked up to the mountains, and over them to the east.

Perhaps it was not all pleasure, so far as I was concerned, but certainly it was all profit. The novels we read were "Tom Jones," in four volumes, and "Clarissa," in its original eight, one or two of Smollett's, and some of Scott's. Rossetti had not, I think, been a great reader of fiction, but his critical judgment was in some respects the surest and soundest I have known. He was one of the only two men I have ever met with who have given me in personal intercourse a sense of the presence of a gift that is above and apart from talent—in a word, of genius. Nothing escaped him. His alert mind seized upon everything. He had never before, I think, given any thought to fiction as an art, but his intellect played over it like a bright light. It amazes me now, after ten years' close study of the methods of story-telling, to recall the general principles which he seemed to formulate out of the back of his head for the defence of his swift verdicts. "Now why?" I would say, when the art of the novelist seemed to me to fail, or when the poet's condemnation appeared extreme. "Because so-and-so *must* happen," he would answer. He was always right. He grasped with masterly strength the operation of the two fundamental factors in the novelist's art—the sympathy and the "tragic mischief." If these were not working well, he knew by the end of the first chapters that, however fine in observation, or racy in humour, or true in pathos, the work as an organism must fail.

It was an education in literary art to sharpen one's wits on such a grindstone, to clarify one's thought in such a stream, to strengthen one's imagination by contact with a mind that was "of imagination all compact."

Now, down to that time, though I had often aspired to the writing of plays, it had never occurred to me that I might write a novel. But I began to think of it then as a remote possibility, and the immediate surroundings of our daily life brought back recollection of the old Cumberland legend. I told the story to Rossetti, and he was impressed by it, but he strongly advised me not to tackle it. The incident did not repel him by its ghastliness, but he saw no way of getting sympathy into it on any side. His judgment disheartened me, and I let the idea go back to the dark chambers of memory. He urged me to try my hand at a Manx story. "'The Bard of Manxland'—it's worth while to be that," he said—he did not know the author of "Foc's'le Yarns." I thought so, too, but the Cumbrian "statesman" had begun to lay hold of my imagination. I had been reviving my recollection and sharpening my practice of the Cumbrian dialect which had been familiar to my ear, and even to my tongue, in childhood, and so my Manx ambitions had to wait.

Two years passed, the poet died, I had spent eighteen months in daily journalism in London, and was then settled in a little bungalow of three rooms in a garden near the beach at Sandown in the Isle of Wight. And there, at length, I began to write my first novel. I had grown impatient of critical work, had persuaded myself (no doubt wrongly) that nobody would go on writing about other people's writing who could do original writing himself, and was resolved to live on little and earn nothing, and never go back to London until I had written something of some sort. As nearly as I can remember, I had enough to keep things going for four months, and if, at the end of that time, nothing had got itself done, I must go back bankrupt.

Something did get done, but at a heavy price of labour and heart-burning. When I began to think of a theme, I found four or five subjects clamouring for acceptance. There was the story of the Prodigal Son, which afterwards became "The Deemster"; the story of Jacob and Esau, which in the same way turned into "The Bondman"; the story of Samuel and Eli, which, after a fashion, moulded itself ultimately into "The Scapegoat"; and half-a-dozen other stories, chiefly Biblical, which are still on the forehead of my time to come. But the Cumbrian legend was first favourite, and to that I addressed myself. I thought I had seen a way to meet Rossetti's objection. The sympathy was to be got out of the elder son. He was to think God's hand was upon him. But whom God's hand rested on had God at his right hand; so the elder son was to be a splendid fellow—brave, strong, calm, patient, long-suffering, a victim of unrequited love, a man standing square on his legs against all weathers. It is said that the young novelist usually begins with a glorified version of his own character; but it must interest my friends to see how every quality of my first hero was a rebuke to my own peculiar infirmities.

Above this central figure and legendary incident I grouped a family of characters. They were heroic and eccentric, good and bad, but they all operated upon the hero. Then I began to write.

Shall I ever forget the agony of the first efforts? There was the ground to clear with necessary explanations. This I did in the way of Scott in a long prefatory chapter. Having written it I read it aloud, and found it unutterably slow and dead. Twenty pages were gone, and the interest was not touched. Throwing the chapter aside I began with an alehouse scene, intending to work back to the history in a piece of retrospective writing. The alehouse was better, but to try its quality I read it aloud, after the "Rainbow" scene in "Silas Marner," and then cast it aside in despair. A third time I began, and when the alehouse looked tolerable the retrospective chapter that followed it seemed flat and poor. How to begin by gripping the interest, how to tell all and yet never stop the action—these were agonising difficulties.

It took me nearly a fortnight to start that novel, sweating drops as of blood at every fresh attempt. I must have written the first half volume four times at the least. After that I saw the way clearer, and got on faster. At the end of three months I had written nearly two volumes, and then in good spirits I went up to London.

My first visit was to J. S. Cotton, an old friend, and to him I detailed the lines of my story. His rapid mind saw a new opportunity. "You want *peine forte et dure*," he said. "What's that?" I said. "An old punishment—a beautiful thing," he answered. "Where's my dear old Blackstone?" and the statute concerning the punishment for standing mute was read to me. It was just the thing I wanted for my hero, and I was in rapture, but I was also in despair. To work this fresh interest into my theme, half of what I had written would need to be destroyed!

It *was* destroyed, the interesting piece of ancient jurisprudence took a leading place in my scheme, and after two months more I got well into the third volume. Then I took my work down to Liverpool, and showed it to my friend, the late John Lovell, a most able man, first manager of the Press Association, but then editing the local *Mercury*. After he had read it he said, "I suppose you want my *candid* opinion?" "Well, ye—s," I said. "It's crude," he said. "But it only wants sub-editing." Sub-editing!

I took it back to London, began again at the first line, and wrote every page over again. At the end of another month the story had been reconstructed, and was shorter by some fifty pages of manuscript. It had drawn my heart's blood to cut out my pet passages, but they were gone, and I knew the book was better. After that I went on to the end and finished with a tragedy. Then the story was sent back to Lovell, and I waited for his verdict.

My home (or what served for it) was now on the fourth floor of New Court, in Lincoln's Inn, and one morning Lovell came purring and blowing and steaming (the good fellow was a twenty-stone man) into my lofty nest. He had re-read my novel coming up in the train. "Well?" I asked, nervously. "It's magnificent," he said. That was all the favourable criticism he offered. All save one practical and tangible bit. "We'll give you 100*l.* for the serial right of the story for the *Weekly*."

He offered one unfavourable criticism. "The death of your hero will never do," he said. "If you kill that man Ralph, you'll kill your book. What's the good? Take no more than the public will give you to begin with, and by-and-by they'll take what *you* give *them*." It was practical advice, but it went sorely against my grain. The death of the hero was the natural sequel to the story; the only end that gave meaning, and intention, and logic to its *motif*. I had a strong predisposition towards a tragic climax to a serious story. To close a narrative of disastrous events with a happy ending it always seemed necessary to turn every incident into accident. That was like laughing at the reader. Comedy was comedy, but comedy and tragedy together was farce. Then a solemn close was so much more impressive. A happy end nearly always frayed off into rags and nothingness, but a sad one closed and clasped a story as with a clasp. Besides, a tragic end might be a glorious and satisfying one, and need by no means be squalid and miserable. But all these arguments went down before my friend's practical assurance: "Kill that man, and you kill your book."

With much diffidence I altered the catastrophe and made my hero happy. Then, thinking my work complete, I asked Mr. Theodore Watts (a friend to whose wise counsel I owed much in those days) to read some "galley" slips of it. He thought the rustic scenes good, but advised me to moderate the dialect, and he propounded to me his well-known views on the use of *patois* in fiction. "It gives a sense of reality," he said, "and often has the effect of wit, but it must not stand in the way." The advice was sound. A man may know over much of his subject to write on it properly. I had studied Cumbrian to too much purpose, and did not realise that some of my scenes were like sealed books to the general reader. So once again I ran over my story, taking out some of the "nobbuts" and the "dustas" and the "wiltas."

My first novel was now written, but I had still to get it published. In my early days in London, while trying to live in the outer court of a calling wherein the struggle for existence is keenest and bitterest and cruellest, I conceived one day the idea of offering myself as a reader to the publishers. With this view I called on several of that ilk, who have perhaps no recollection of my early application. I recall my interview with one of them. He was sitting at a table when I was taken into his room, and he never once raised his head from his papers to look at me. I just remember that he had a neck like a three-decker, and a voice like a peahen's. "Well, sir?" he said. I mentioned the object of my visit. "What can you read?" "Novels and poems," I answered. "Don't publish either—good day," he said, and I went out.

But one of the very best, and quite, I think, the very oldest of publishers now living, received me differently. "Come into my own room," he said. It was a lovely little place, full of an atmosphere that recalled the publishing house of the old days, half office, half study; a workshop where books might be made, not turned out by machinery. I read many manuscripts for that publisher, and must have learned much by the experience. And now that my novel was finished I took it to him first. He offered to publish it the following year. That did not suit me, and I took my book elsewhere. Next day I was offered 50*l.* for my copyright. That was wages at the rate of about four shillings a day for the time I had been actually engaged upon the work, sweating brain and heart and every faculty. Nevertheless, one of my friends urged me to accept it. "Why?" I asked. "Because it is a story of the past, and therefore not one publisher in ten will look at it." I used strong language, and then took my novel to Chatto & Windus. Within a few hours Mr. Chatto made me an offer which I accepted. The book is now, I think, in its fifteenth edition.

The story I have told of many breakdowns in the attempt to write my first novel may suggest the idea that I was merely serving my apprenticeship to fiction. It is true that I was, but it would be wrong to conclude that the writing of a novel has been plain sailing with me ever since. Let me "throw a crust to my critics," and confess that I am serving my apprenticeship still. Every book that I have written since has offered yet greater difficulties. Not one of the little series but has at some moment been a despair to me. There has always been a point of the story at which I have felt confident that it must kill me. I have written six novels (that is to say, about sixteen), and sworn as many oaths that I would never begin another. Three times I have thrown up commissions in sheer terror of the work ahead of one. Yet here I am at this moment (like half-a-dozen of my fellow-craftsmen), with contracts in hand which I cannot get through for three years. The public expects a novel to be light reading. It may revenge itself for occasional disappointments by remembering that a novel is not always light writing.

Let me conclude with a few words that may be timely. Of all the literary cants that I despise and hate, the one I hate and despise the most is that which would have the world believe that greatly gifted men who have become distinguished in literature and are earning thousands a year by it, and have no public existence and no apology apart from it, hold it in pity as a profession and in contempt as an art. For my own part, I have found the profession of letters a serious pursuit, of which in no company and in no country have I had need to be ashamed. It has demanded all my powers, fired all my enthusiasm, developed my sympathies, enlarged my friendships, touched, amused, soothed, and comforted me. If it has been hard work, it has also been a constant inspiration, and I would not change it for all the glory and more than all the emoluments of the best-paid and the most illustrious profession in the world.

"The Social Kaleidoscope"

By George R. Sims

My first book hardly deserved the title. I have only a dim remembrance of it now, because it is one of those things which I have studiously set myself to forget. I was very proud of it before I saw it. After I had seen it, I realised in one swift moment's anguish the concentrated truth of the word vanity as applied to human wishes. Hidden away in the bottom corner of an old box, which is not to be opened until after I am dead, that first book lies at the present moment; that is to say, unless the process of decay, which had already set in upon the paper on which it was printed, has gone on to the bitter end, and the book has disappeared entirely of its own accord.

Before that book was published, I used to lie awake at night and fancy how great and how grand a thing it would be for me to see a book with my name on the cover lying on Smith's bookstalls, and staring me in the face from the booksellers' windows. After it was published, I felt that I owed Messrs. Smith & Sons a deep debt of gratitude for refusing to take it, and my heart rejoiced within me greatly that the only booksellers who exhibited it lived principally in old back streets and half-finished suburban thoroughfares.

Stay—I will go upstairs to my lumber room, I will open that box, I will dig deep down among the buried memories of the past, and I will find that book, and I will summon up my courage and ask the publishers of this volume to kindly allow the cover of that book to be reproduced here. It is only by looking at it as I looked at it that you will thoroughly appreciate my feelings on the subject.

I have found the box, but my heart sinks within me as I try to open the lid. All my lost youth lies there. The key is rusty and will hardly turn in the lock.

So—so—so, at last! Ghosts of the long ago, come forth from your resting-places and haunt me once again.

Dear me! dear me! how musty everything smells; how old, and worn, and time-stained everything is. A folded poster:

"Mr. G. R. Sims will positively *not* appear this evening at the entertainment held in the Hall."

Yes, I remember. I had been announced, entirely without my consent or knowledge, to appear at a hall attached to the Grecian Theatre with Mrs. Georgina Weldon, and take part in an entertainment. This notice was stuck about outside the theatre in consequence of my indignant remonstrance. My old friend Mr. George Conquest had, I need hardly say, nothing to do with that bill. Someone had taken the hall for a special occasion. I think it was something remotely connected with lunatics.

My first play! Poor little play—a burlesque written for my brothers and sisters, and played by us in the Theatre Royal Day Nursery. There were some really brilliant lines in it, I remember. They were taken bodily from a burlesque of H. J. Byron's, which I purchased at Lacy & Son's (now French's) in the Strand—"a new and original burlesque by Master G. R. Sims." My misguided parents actually had the playbill printed and invited friends to witness the performance. They little knew what they were doing by pandering to my boyish vanity in such a way. But for that printed playbill, and that public performance in my nursery, I might never have taken to the stage, and inflicted upon a long-suffering public Adelphi melodrama and Gaiety burlesque, farcical comedy and comic opera; I might have remained all my life an honest, hard-working City man, relieving my feelings occasionally by joining in the autumn discussions in the *Daily Telegraph*. I was still in the City when my first book was published. I used, in those days, to get to the City at nine and leave it at six, but I had a dinner hour, and in that dinner hour I wrote short stories and little things that I fancied were funny, and I used to put them in big envelopes and send them to the different magazines. I sent about twenty out in that way. I never had one accepted, but several returned.

I wrote my first book in my dinner hour, in a City office. I have just found it. Here is the cover. You will observe that it has my portrait on it. I look very ill and thin and haggard. That was, perhaps, the result of going without my dinner in order to devote myself to "literature."

If you could look inside that book, if you could see the paper on which it is printed, you would understand the shock it was to me when they laid it in my arms and said: "Behold your firstborn."

All the vanity in me (and they tell me that I have a good deal) rose up as I gazed at the battered wreck upon the cover—the man with the face that suggested a prompt subscription to a burial club.

But I shouldn't have minded that so much if the people who bought my book hadn't written to me personally to complain. One gentleman sent me a postcard to say that his volume fell to pieces while he was carrying it home. Another assured me that he had picked enough pieces of straw out of the leaves to make a bed for his horse with, and a third returned a copy to me without paying the postage, and asked me kindly to put it in *my* dustbin, because his cook was rather proud of the one he had in his back garden.

Still the book sold (the sketches had all previously appeared in the *Weekly Dispatch*), and when the first edition was exhausted, a new and better one was prepared (without that haggard face upon the cover), and I was happy.

The sale ran into thirty thousand the first year of publication, and as I was fortunate enough to have published it on a royalty, I am glad to say it is still selling.

"The Social Kaleidoscope" was my first book. With it I made my actual *début* between covers.

I hadn't done very well before then; since then I have, from a worldly point of view, done remarkably well—far better than I deserved to do, my good-natured friends assure me, and I cordially agree with them.

But I had made a good fight for it, and I had suffered years of disappointment and rebuff. I began to send contributions to periodicals when I was fourteen years old, and a boy at Hanwell College. *Fun* was the first journal I favoured with my effusions, and week after week I had a sinking at the heart as I bought that popular periodical and searched in vain for my comic verses, my humorous sketches, and my smart paragraphs.

It took me thirteen years to get something printed and paid for, but I succeeded at last, and it was *Fun*, my early love, that first took me by the hand. When I was on the staff of *Fun*, and its columns were open to me for all I cared to write, I used often to look over the batch of boyish efforts that littered the editor's desk, and let my heart go out to the writers who were suffering the pangs that I had known so well.

I had had effusions of mine printed before that, but I didn't get any money for them. I had the pleasure of seeing my signature more than once in the columns of certain theatrical journals, in the days when I was a constant first-nighter, and a determined upholder of the privileges of the pit. And I even had some of my poetry printed. In the old box to which I have gone in search of the first edition of my first book, there are two papers carefully preserved, because they were once my pride and glory. One is a copy of the *Halfpenny Journal*, and the other is a copy of the *Halfpenny Welcome Guest*. On the back page of the correspondence column of the former there is a poem signed "G. R. S.," addressed to a young lady's initials in affectionately complimentary terms. Alas! I don't know what has become of that young lady. Probably she is married, and is the mother of a fine family of boys and girls, and has forgotten that I ever wrote verses in her honour. I think I sent her a copy of the *Halfpenny Journal*, but a few weeks after a coldness sprang up between us. She was behind the counter of a confectioner's shop in Camden Town, and I found her one afternoon giggling at a young friend of mine who used to buy his butterscotch there. My friend and I had words, but between myself and that fair confectioner "the rest was silence."

I was really very much distressed that my pride compelled me never again to cross the threshold of that establishment. There wasn't a confectioner's in all Camden Town that could come within measurable distance of it for strawberry ices.

In the correspondence column of the *Halfpenny Welcome Guest*, which is among my buried treasures, there is an "answer" instead of the poem which I had fondly hoped to see inserted in its glorious pages. And this is the answer: "G. R. S.—Your poem is not quite up to our standard, but it gives decided promise of better things. We should advise you to persevere."

I am quoting from memory, for after turning that box upside down, I can't lay my hand on this particular *Welcome Guest*, though I know that it is there. I don't know who the editor was who gave me that kindly pat on the head, but whoever he was he earned my undying gratitude. At the time I felt I should have liked him better had he printed my poem. I was no more fortunate with my prose than I was with my poetry. I began to tell stories at a very early age, but it was not until after I had succeeded in getting a poem printed among the "Answers to Correspondents" that I took seriously to prose with a view of publication. I was encouraged to try my hand at writing stories by the remembrance of the success which had attended my efforts at romantic narrative when I was a school-boy.

There were eight other boys in the dormitory I slept in at Hanwell (the College, not the Asylum), and they used to make me tell them stories every night until they fell asleep, and woe betide me if I cut my narrative short while one of them remained awake. I wasn't much of a boy with a bolster or a boot, but they were all champions, and many a time when I had married the hero and heroine and wound up my story did I have to start a fresh complication in a hurry to save myself from chastisement. I remember on one occasion, when I was dreadfully sleepy, and I had got into a fearful fog as to who committed the murder, I made a wild plunge at a ghost to get me out of the difficulty, and the whole dormitory rose to a boy and set about me with bolsters in their indignation at such a lame and impotent conclusion.

Night after night did those maddening words, "Tell us a story," salute my ears as I laid my weary little head upon the pillow, and I had to tell one or run the gauntlet of eight bolsters and sixteen slippers, to say nothing of the biggest boy of all, who kept a reserve pair of boots hidden away under his bed for purposes not altogether unconnected with midnight excursions to a neighbouring orchard.

It was the remembrance of my early story-telling days that prompted me, when poetry seemed a drug in the market, to try my hand at what is now, I believe, called "The Complete Novelette."

I set myself seriously to work, laid in a large stock of apples and jumbles, and spent several consecutive afternoons in completing a story which I called "A Pleasant Evening." After I had written it I copied it out in my best hand, and then, with fear and trembling, I sent it to the *Family Herald*.

I sent it to the *Family Herald* because I had heard a lady who visited at our house say that she knew a lady who knew a lady who had sent a story to the *Family Herald*, never having written anything before in her life, and the story had been accepted, and the writer had received five pounds for it by return of post.

I didn't receive anything by return of post, but in about a fortnight my manuscript came back to me. Nothing daunted, I carefully cut off the corner on which "Declined with thanks" had been written, and I sent the story to *Chamber's Journal*. Here it met with a similar fate, but I fancy it took a little longer to come back, and it bore signs of wear and tear. I knew, or I had read, that it was not wise to let your manuscript have the appearance of being rejected, so I spent several unpleasant evenings in writing "A Pleasant Evening" out again, and I sent it to *All the Year Round*.

It came back! This time I didn't take the trouble to open it I knew it directly I saw it, and as it reached me so I flung it in my desk and bit my lips, and made up my mind that after all it was better to be accepted as a poet in the "Answers to Correspondents" column of the *Halfpenny Journal* than to be rejected as a story-writer by the editors of higher-priced periodicals.

But though I played with poetry again, I didn't even succeed in getting into the "Answers to Correspondents." My vaulting ambition o'erleaped its selle, and I sent my verses to journals which didn't "correspond." In those days I kept a little book, in which I entered all the manuscripts I sent to editors, and from it now I copy the following instructive record. R stands for "Returned":—

Once a Week	"The Minstrel's Curse"	R.
Belgravia	"After the Battle"	R.
Broadway	"After the Battle"	R.
Fun	"Nearer and Dearer"	R.
Fun	"An Unfortunate Attachment"	R.
Fun	"A Song of May"	R.
Banter	"Nearer and Dearer"	R.
Judy	"An Unfortunate Attachment"	R.
London Society	"The Minstrel's Curse"	R.
Owl	"Nearer and Dearer"	R.

Returned! Returned! Returned! All I got for my pains was the chance of making a joke in my diary on my birthday. In those days of my wild struggles with Fate I find written against the 2nd of September, "Many unhappy Returns."

I believe that I should have flung up authorship in despair, and never have had a first book, but for the chance remark of the dear old doctor who looked after my health in the days when I hadn't to pay my own doctor's bills.

He was talking about me one day in my father's private office, and I happened to be passing, and I heard him say, "He's a nice lad—what a pity he scribbles!" Scribbles! the word burnt itself into my brain, it seared my heart, it brought the hot blood to my cheeks, and the indignant tears to my eyes. Was I not ready to write an acrostic at a moment's notice on the name of the sweetheart of any fellow who asked me to do it? Had I not written a poem on the fall of Napoleon, which my eldest sister had read aloud to her schoolfellows, and made them all mad with jealousy to think there wasn't a brother among the lot of them who could even rhyme decently? Had I not had stories rejected by the *Family Herald*, *All the Year Round*, and *Chambers's Journal*, and a letter on the subject of the crossing opposite St. Mark's Church, Hamilton Terrace, printed in the *Marylebone Mercury*? And was I to be dubbed a scribbler, and pitied for my weakness? It is nearly twenty years since those words were uttered, and my dear old doctor rests beyond the reach of all human ills, but I can hear them now. They have never ceased to ring in my ears as they rang that day.

My pride was wounded, my vanity was hurt, I was put upon my mettle. I registered a silent vow there and then that some day I would have a noble revenge on my friendly detractor, and make him confess that he was wrong when he said that it was a pity I scribbled.

From that hour I set myself steadily to be an author. I wrote poetry by the mile, prose by the acre, and I sent it to every kind of periodical that I could find in the "Post Office Directory."

I had to pass through years of rejection, but still I wrote on, and still I spent all my pocket-money on books, and postage-stamps, and paper.

And at last the chance came. I was allowed to write paragraphs in the *Weekly Dispatch* by a friend who was a real journalist, and had a column at his disposal to fill with gossip.

After doing the work for a month for nothing, I had the whole column given to me, and one day I received my first guinea earned by scribbling.

I was a proud man when I went out of the *Dispatch* office that day with a sovereign and a shilling in my hand. I had forced the gates of the citadel at last. I had marched in with the honours of war, and I was marching out with the price of victory in my hand.

Soon afterwards there came another chance. The editor of the *Dispatch* wanted a series of short complete stories. I asked to be allowed to try if I could do them. Under the title of "The Social Kaleidoscope," I wrote a series of short stories or sketches, and from that day no week has passed that I have not contributed something to the columns of a weekly journal.

When the sketches were complete, the publisher of the *Dispatch* offered to bring them out in book form for me and publish them in the office.

"The Social Kaleidoscope" was my first book, and that is how it came into the world.

Years afterwards, my chance came with the dear old fellow who had said that it was a pity I scribbled so. Fortune had smiled upon me in one way then, and I was earning an excellent income with my pen. But my health had broken down, and it was thought necessary that I should place myself in the hands of a celebrated surgeon. I had not seen my old doctor for some years, but my people wished that he should be consulted, because he had known me so well in the days of my youth.

So I submitted, and he came, and he shook his head and agreed that so-and-so was the man to take me in hand.

"I think he'll cure you, my dear fellow," said the doctor; "he's the most skilful surgeon we have for cases like yours, but his fee is a heavy one. Still, you can afford it."

"Yes, doctor," I replied, "thanks to my *scribbling*, I can."

That was the hour of my triumph. I had waited for it for fifteen years, but it had come at last.

The dear old boy gripped my hand. "I was wrong," he said, with a quiet smile, "and I confess it; but we'll get you well, and you shall scribble for many a year to come."

And I am scribbling still.

"Departmental Ditties"

By Rudyard Kipling

As there is only one man in charge of a steamer, so there is but one man in charge of a newspaper, and he is the editor. My chief taught me this on an Indian journal, and he further explained that an order was an order, to be obeyed at a run, not a walk, and that any notion or notions as to the fitness or unfitness of any particular kind of work for the young had better be held over till the last page was locked up to press. He was breaking me into harness, and I owe him a deep debt of gratitude, which I did not discharge at the time. The path of virtue was very steep, whereas the writing of verses allowed a certain play to the mind, and, unlike the filling in of reading matter, could be done as the spirit served. Now, a sub-editor is not hired to write verses: he is paid to sub-edit. At the time, this discovery shocked me greatly; but, some years later, when I came to be a sort of an editor in charge, Providence dealt me for my subordinate one saturated with Elia. He wrote very pretty, Lamblike essays, but he wrote them when he should have been sub-editing. Then I saw a little of what my chief must have suffered on my account. There is a moral here for the ambitious and aspiring who are oppressed by their superiors.

This is a digression, as all my verses were digressions from office work. They came without invitation, unmanneredly, in the nature of things; but they had to come, and the writing out of them kept me healthy and amused. To the best of my remembrance, no one then discovered their grievous cynicism, or their pessimistic tendency, and I was far too busy, and too happy, to take thought about these things.

So they arrived merrily, being born out of the life about me, and they were very bad indeed, and the joy of doing them was payment a thousand times their worth. Some, of course, came and ran away again, and the dear sorrow of going in search of these (out of office hours, and catching them) was almost better than writing them clear. Bad as they were, I burned twice as many as were published, and of the survivors at least two-thirds were cut down at the last moment. Nothing can be wholly beautiful that is not useful, and therefore my verses were made to ease off the perpetual strife between the manager extending his advertisements and my chief fighting for his reading-matter. They were born to be sacrificed. Rukn-Din, the foreman of our side, approved of them immensely, for he was a Muslim of culture. He would say: "Your potery very good, sir; just coming proper length today. You giving more soon? One-third column just proper. Always can take on third page."

Mahmoud, who set them up, had an unpleasant way of referring to a new lyric as "*Ek aur chiz*"—one more thing—which I never liked. The job side, too, were unsympathetic, because I used to raid into their type for private proofs with old English and Gothic headlines. Even a Hindoo does not like to find the serifs of his f's cut away to make long s's.

And in this manner, week by week, my verses came to be printed in the paper. I was in very good company, for there is always an undercurrent of song, a little bitter for the most part, running through the Indian papers. The bulk of it is much better than mine, being more graceful, and is done by those less than Sir Alfred Lyall— to whom I would apologise for mentioning his name in this gallery— "Pekin," "Latakia," "Cigarette," "O.," "T. W.," "Foresight," and others, whose names come up with the stars out of the Indian Ocean going eastward.

Sometimes a man in Bangalore would be moved to song, and a man on the Bombay side would answer him, and a man in Bengal would echo back, till at last we would all be crowing together like cocks before daybreak, when it is too dark to see your fellow. And, occasionally, some unhappy Chaaszee, away in the China Ports, would lift up his voice among the tea-chests, and the queer-smelling yellow papers of the Far East brought us his sorrows. The newspaper files showed that, forty years ago, the men sang of just the same subjects as we did—of heat, loneliness, love, lack of promotion, poverty, sport, and war. Further back still, at the end of the eighteenth century, Hickey's *Bengal Gazette*, a very wicked little sheet in Calcutta, published the songs of the young factors, ensigns, and writers to the East India Company. They, too, wrote of the same things, but in those days men were strong enough to buy a bullock's heart for dinner, cook it with their own hands because they could not afford a servant, and make a rhymed jest of all the squalor and poverty. Lives were not worth two monsoons' purchase, and perhaps the knowledge of this a little coloured the rhymes when they sang:

> *In a very short time you're released from all cares—*
> *If the Padri's asleep, Mr. Oldham reads prayers!*

The note of physical discomfort that runs through so much Anglo-Indian poetry had been struck then. You will find it most fully suggested in "The Long, Long Indian Day," a comparatively modern affair; but there is a set of verses called "Scanty Ninety-five," dated about Warren Hastings's time, which gives a lively idea of what our seniors in the Service had to put up with. One of the most interesting poems I ever found was written at Meerut, three or four days before the Mutiny broke out there. The author complained that he could not get his clothes washed nicely that week, and was very facetious over his worries.

My verses had the good fortune to last a little longer than someothers, which were more true to facts and certainly better workmanship. Men in the Army, and the Civil Service, and the Railway, wrote to me saying that the rhymes might be made into a book. Some of them had been sung to the banjoes round camp fires, and some had run as far down coast as Rangoon and Moulmein, and up to Mandalay. A real book was out of the question, but I knew that Rukn-Din and the office plant were at my disposal at a price, if I did not use the office time. Also, I had handled in the previous year a couple of small books, of which I was part owner, and had lost nothing. So there was built a sort of a book, a lean oblong docket, wire-stitched, to imitate a D.O. Government envelope, printed on one side only, bound in brown paper, and secured with red tape. It was addressed to all heads of departments and all Government officials, and among a pile of papers would have deceived a clerk of twenty years' service. Of these "books" we made some hundreds, and as there was no necessity for advertising, my public being to my hand, I took reply-postcards, printed the news of the birth of the book on one side, the blank order-form on the other, and posted them up and down the Empire from Aden to Singapore, and from Quetta to Colombo. There was no trade discount, no reckoning twelves as thirteens, no commission, and no credit of any kind whatever. The money came back in poor but honest rupees, and was transferred from the publisher, the left-hand pocket, direct to the author, the right-hand pocket. Every copy sold in a few weeks, and the ratio of expenses to profits, as I remember it, has since prevented my injuring my health by sympathising with publishers who talk of their risks and advertisements. The down-country papers complained of the form of the thing. The wire binding cut the pages, and the red tape tore the covers. This was not intentional, but Heaven helps those who help themselves. Consequently, there arose a demand for a new edition, and this time I exchanged the pleasure of taking in money over the counter for that of seeing a real publisher's imprint on the title-page. More verses were taken out and put in, and some of that edition travelled as far as Hong-Kong on the map, and each edition grew a little fatter, and, at last, the book came to London with a gilt top and a stiff back, and was advertised in the publishers' poetry department.

But I loved it best when it was a little brown baby with a pink string round its stomach; a child's child, ignorant that it was afflicted with all the most modern ailments; and before people had learned, beyond doubt, how its author lay awake of nights in India, plotting and scheming to write something that should "take" with the English public.

JUVENILIA

By A. Conan Doyle

It is very well for the master craftsman with twenty triumphs behind him to look down the vista of his successes, and to recall how he picked out the path which has led him to fame, but for the tiro whose first book is perilously near to his last one it becomes a more invidious matter. His past presses too closely upon his present, and his reminiscences, unmellowed by the flight of years, are apt to be rawly and crudely personal. And yet even time helps me when I speak of my first work, for it was written seven-and-twenty years ago.

I was six at the time, and have a very distinct recollection of the achievement It was written, I remember, upon foolscap paper, in what might be called a fine bold hand—four words to the line, and was illustrated by marginal pen-and-ink sketches by the author. There was a man in it, and there was a tiger. I forget which was the hero, but it didn't matter much, for they became blended into one about the time when the tiger met the man. I was a realist in the age of the Romanticists. I described at some length, both verbally and pictorially, the untimely end of that wayfarer. But when the tiger had absorbed him, I found myself slightly embarrassed as to how my story was to go on. "It is very easy to get people into scrapes, and very hard to get them out again," I remarked, and I have often had cause to repeat the precocious aphorism of my childhood. On this occasion the situation was beyond me, and my book, like my man, was engulfed in my tiger. There is an old family bureau with secret drawers, in which lie little locks of hair tied up in circles, and black silhouettes and dim daguerreotypes, and letters which seem to have been written in the lightest of straw-coloured inks. Somewhere there lies my primitive manuscript, where my tiger, like a many-hooped barrel with a tail to it, still envelops the hapless stranger whom he has taken in.

Then came my second book, which was told and not written, but which was a much more ambitious effort than the first. Between the two, four years had elapsed, which were mainly spent in reading. It is rumoured that a special meeting of a library committee was held in my honour, at which a bye-law was passed that no subscriber should be permitted to change his book more than three times a day. Yet, even with these limitations, by the aid of a well-stocked bookcase at home, I managed to enter my tenth year with a good deal in my head that I could never have learned in the class-rooms.

I do not think that life has any joy to offer so complete, so soul-filling as that which comes upon the imaginative lad, whose spare time is limited, but who is able to snuggle down into a corner with his book, knowing that the next hour is all his own. And how vivid and fresh it all is! Your very heart and soul are out on the prairies and the oceans with your hero. It is you who act and suffer and enjoy. You carry the long small-bore Kentucky rifle with which such egregious things are done, and you lie out upon the topsail yard, and get jerked by the flap of the sail into the Pacific, where you cling on to the leg of an albatross, and so keep afloat until the comic boatswain turns up with his crew of volunteers to handspike you into safety. What a magic it is, this stirring of the boyish heart and mind! Long ere I came to my teens I had traversed every sea and knew the Rockies like my own back garden. How often had I sprung upon the back of the charging buffalo and so escaped him! It was an everyday emergency to have to set the prairie on fire in front of me in order to escape from the fire behind, or to run a mile down a brook to throw the bloodhounds off my trail. I had creased horses, I had shot down rapids, I had strapped on my mocassins hind-foremost to conceal my tracks, I had lain under water with a reed in my mouth, and I had feigned madness to escape the torture. As to the Indian braves whom I slew in single combats, I could have stocked a large graveyard, and, fortunately enough, though I was a good deal chipped about in these affairs, no real harm ever came of it, and I was always nursed back into health by a very fascinating young squaw. It was all more real than the reality. Since those days I have in very truth both shot bears and harpooned whales, but the performance was flat compared with the first time that I did it with Mr. Ballantyne or Captain Mayne Reid at my elbow.

In the fulness of time I was packed off to a public school, and in some way it was discovered by my playmates that I had more than my share of the lore after which they hankered. There was my *début* as a story-teller. On a wet half-holiday I have been elevated on to a desk, and with an audience of little boys all squatting on the floor, with their chins upon their hands, I have talked myself husky over the misfortunes of my heroes. Week in and week out those unhappy men have battled and striven and groaned for the amusement of that little circle. I was bribed with pastry to continue these efforts, and I remember that I always stipulated for tarts down and strict business, which shows that I was born to be a member of the Authors' Society. Sometimes, too, I would stop dead in the very thrill of a crisis, and could only be set agoing again by apples. When I had got as far as "With his left hand in her glossy locks, he was waving the blood-stained knife above her head, when—" or "Slowly, slowly, the door turned upon its hinges, and with eyes which were dilated with horror, the wicked Marquis saw—" I knew that I had my audience in my power. And thus my second book was evolved.

It may be that my literary experiences would have ended there had there not come a time in my early manhood when that good old harsh-faced schoolmistress, Hard Times, took me by the hand. I wrote, and with amazement I found that my writing was accepted. *Chambers's Journal* it was which rose to the occasion, and I have had a kindly feeling for its mustard-coloured back ever since. Fifty little cylinders of manuscript did I send out during eight years, which described irregular orbits among publishers, and usually came back like paper boomerangs to the place that they had started from. Yet in time they all lodged somewhere or other. Mr. Hogg, of *London Society*, was one of the most constant of my patrons, and Mr. James Payn wasted hours of his valuable time in encouraging me to persevere. Knowing as I did that he was one of the busiest men in London, I never received one of his shrewd and kindly and most illegible letters without a feeling of gratitude and wonder.

I have heard folk talk as though there were some hidden back door by which one may creep into literature, but I can say myself that I never had an introduction to any editor or publisher before doing business with them, and that I do not think that I suffered on that account. Yet my apprenticeship was a long and trying one. During ten years of hard work, I averaged less than fifty pounds a year from my pen. I won my way into the best journals, *Cornhill*, *Temple Bar*, and so on; but what is the use of that when the contributions to those journals must be anonymous? It is a system which tells very hardly against young authors. I saw with astonishment and pride that "Habakuk Jephson's Statement" in the *Cornhill* was attributed by critic after critic to Stevenson, but, overwhelmed as I was by the compliment, a word of the most lukewarm praise sent straight to my own address would have been of greater use to me. After ten years of such work I was as unknown as if I had never dipped a pen into an ink-bottle. Sometimes, of course, the anonymous system may screen you from blame as well as rob you of praise. How well I can see a dear old friend running after me in the street, waving a London evening paper in his hand! "Have you seen what they say about your *Cornhill* story?" he shouted. "No, no. What is it?" "Here it is! Here it is!" Eagerly he turned over the column, while I, trembling with excitement, but determined to bear my honours meekly, peeped over his shoulder. "The *Cornhill* this month," said the critic, "has a story in it which would have made Thackeray turn in his grave." There were several witnesses about, and the Portsmouth bench are severe upon assaults, so my friend escaped unscathed. Then first I realised that British criticism had fallen into a shocking state of decay, though when someone has a pat on the back for you you understand that, after all, there are some very smart people upon the literary Press.

And so at last it was brought home to me that a man may put the very best that is in him into magazine work for years and years and reap no benefit from it, save, of course, the inherent benefits of literary practice. So I wrote another of my first books and sent it off to the publishers. Alas for the dreadful thing that happened! The publishers never received it, the Post Office sent countless blue forms to say that they knew nothing about it, and from that day to this no word has ever been heard of it. Of course it was the best thing I ever wrote. Who ever lost a manuscript that wasn't? But I must in all honesty confess that my shock at its disappearance would be as nothing to my horror if it were suddenly to appear again—in print. If one or two other of my earlier efforts had also been lost in the post, my conscience would have been the lighter. This one was called "The Narrative of John Smith," and it was of a personal-social-political complexion. Had it appeared I should have probably awakened to find myself infamous, for it steered, as I remember it, perilously near to the libellous. However, it was safely lost, and that was the end of another of my first books.

Then I started upon an exceedingly sensational novel, which interested me extremely at the time, though I have never heard that it had the same effect upon anyone else afterwards. I may urge in extenuation of all shortcomings that it was written in the intervals of a busy though ill-paying practice. And a man must try that and combine it with literary work before he quite knows what it means. How often have I rejoiced to find a clear morning before me, and settled down to my task, or rather, dashed ferociously at it, as knowing how precious were those hours of quiet! Then to me enter my housekeeper, with tidings of dismay. "Mrs. Thurston's little boy wants to see you, doctor." "Show him in," say I, striving to fix my scene in my mind that I may splice it when this trouble is over. "Well, my boy?" "Please, doctor, mother wants to know if she is to add water to that medicine." "Certainly, certainly." Not that it matters in the least, but it is well to answer with decision. Exit the little boy, and the splice is about half accomplished when he suddenly bursts into the room again. "Please, doctor, when I got back mother had taken the medicine without the water." "Tut, tut!" I answer. "It really does not matter in the least." The youth withdraws with a suspicious glance, and one more paragraph has been written when the husband puts in an appearance. "There seems to have been some misunderstanding about that medicine," he remarks coldly. "Not at all," I say, "it really didn't matter." "Well, then, why did you tell the boy that it should be taken with water?" And then I try to disentangle the business, and the husband shakes his head gloomily at me. "She feels very queer," says he; "we should all be easier in our minds if you came and looked at her." So I leave my heroine in the four-foot way with an express thundering towards her, and trudge sadly off, with the feeling that another morning has been wasted, and another seam left visible to the critic's eye in my unhappy novel. Such was the genesis of my sensational romance, and when publishers wrote to say that they could see no merit in it, I was, heart and soul, of the same way of thinking.

And then, under more favourable circumstances, I wrote "Micah Clarke," for patients had become more tractable, and I had married, and in every way I was a brighter man. A year's reading and five months' writing finished it, and I thought I had a tool in my hands that would cut a path for me. So I had, but the first thing that I cut with it was my finger. I sent it to a friend, whose opinion I deeply respected, in London, who read for one of the leading houses, but he had been bitten by the historical novel, and very naturally he distrusted it. From him it went to house after house, and house after house would have none of it. Blackwood found that the people did not talk so in the seventeenth century; Bentley that its principal defect was that there was a complete absence of interest; Cassells that experience had shown that an historical novel could never be a commercial success. I remember smoking over my dog-eared manuscript when it returned for a whiff of country air after one of its descents upon town, and wondering what I should do if some sporting, reckless kind of publisher were suddenly to stride in and make me a bid of forty shillings or so for the lot. And then suddenly I bethought me to send it to Messrs. Longmans, where it was fortunate enough to fall into the hands of Mr. Andrew Lang. From that day the way was smoothed to it, and, as things turned out, I was spared that keenest sting of ill-success, that those who had believed in your work should suffer pecuniarily for their belief. A door had been opened for me into the temple of the Muses, and it only remained that I should find something that was worthy of being borne through it.

"The Trail of the Serpent"

By M. E. Braddon

My first novel! Far back in the distinctness of childish memories I see a little girl who has lately learnt to write, who has lately been given a beautiful brand-new mahogany desk, with a red velvet slope, and a glass ink-bottle, such a desk as might now be bought for three-and-sixpence, but which in the forties cost at least half a guinea. Very proud is the little girl, with the Kenwigs pigtails and the Kenwigs frills, of that mahogany desk, and its infinite capacities for literary labour, above all, gem of gems, its stick of variegated sealing-wax, brown, speckled with gold, and its little glass seal with an intaglio representing two doves—Pliny's doves, perhaps, famous in mosaic, only the little girl had never heard of Pliny, or his Laurentine Villa.

Armed with that desk and its supply of stationery, Mary Elizabeth Braddon—very fond of writing her name at full length, and her address also at full length, though the word "Middlesex" offered difficulties—began that pilgrimage on the broad high road of fiction, which was destined to be a longish one. So much for the little girl of eight years old, in the third person, and now to become strictly autobiographical.

My first story was based on those fairy tales which first opened to me the world of imaginative literature. My first attempt in fiction, and in round-hand, on carefully pencilled double lines, was a story of two sisters, a good sister and a wicked, and I fear adhered more faithfully to the lines of the archetypal story than the writer's pen kept to the double fence which should have ensured neatness.

The interval between the ages of eight and twelve was a prolific period, fertile in unfinished MSS., among which I can now trace an historical novel on the Siege of Calais, an Eastern story, suggested by a passionate love of Miss Pardoe's Turkish tales, and Byron's "Bride of Abydos," which my mother, a devoted Byron worshipper, allowed me to read aloud to her—and doubtless murder in the reading—a story of the Hartz Mountains, with audacious flights in German diablerie; and lastly, very seriously undertaken, and very perseveringly worked upon, a domestic story, the outline of which was suggested by the same dear and sympathetic mother.

Now it is a curious fact, which may or may not be common to other story-spinners, that I have never been able to take kindly to a plot—or the suggestion of a plot—offered to me by anybody else. The moment a friend tells me that he or she is desirous of imparting a series of facts—strictly true—as if truth in fiction mattered one jot!—which in his or her opinion would make the ground plan of an admirable, startling, and altogether original three-volume novel, I know in advance that my imagination will never grapple with those startling circumstances—that my thoughts will begin to wander before my friend has got half through the remarkable chain of events, and that if the obliging purveyor of romantic incidents were to examine me at the end of the story, I should be spun ignominiously. For the most part, such subjects as have been proposed to me by friends have been hopelessly unfit for the circulating library; or, where not immoral, have been utterly dull; but it is, I believe, a fixed idea in the novel-reader's mind that any combination of events out of the beaten way of life will make an admirable subject for the novelist's art.

My dear mother, taking into consideration my tender years, and perhaps influenced in somewise by her own love of picking up odd bits of Sheraton or Chippendale furniture in the storehouses of the less ambitious second-hand dealers of those simpler days, offered me the following *scenario* for a domestic story. It was an incident which, I doubt not, she had often read at the tail of a newspaper column, and which certainly savours of the gigantic gooseberry, the sea-serpent, and the agricultural labourer who unexpectedly inherits half a million. It was eminently a Simple Story, and far more worthy of that title than Mrs. Inchbald's long and involved romance.

An honest couple, in humble circumstances, possess among their small household gear a good old easy chair, which has been the pride of a former generation, and is the choicest of their household gods. A comfortable cushioned chair, snug and restful, albeit the chintz covering, though clean and tidy, as virtuous people's furniture always is in fiction, is worn thin by long service, while the dear chair itself is no longer the chair it once was as to legs and framework.

Evil days come upon the praiseworthy couple and their dependent brood, among whom I faintly remember the love interest of the story to have lain; and that direful day arrives when the average landlord of juvenile fiction, whose heart is of adamant and brain of brass, distrains for the rent. The rude broker swoops upon the humble dovecot; a cart or hand-barrow waits on the carefully hearth-stoned doorstep for the household gods; the family gather round the cherished chair, on which the rude broker has already laid his grimy fingers; they hang over the back and fondle the padded arms; and the old grandmother, with clasped hands, entreats that, if able to raise the money in a few days, they may be allowed to buy back that loved heirloom.

The broker laughs the plea to scorn; they might have their chair, and cheap enough, he had no doubt. The cover was darned and patched—as only the virtuous poor of fiction do darn and do patch—and he made no doubt the stuffing was nothing better than brown wool; and with that coarse taunt the coarser broker dug his clasp-knife into the cushion against which grandfatherly backs had leaned in happier days, and lo! an avalanche of banknotes fell out of the much-maligned horsehair, and the family was lifted from penury to wealth. Nothing more simple—or more natural. A prudent but eccentric ancestor had chosen this mode of putting by his savings, assured that, whenever discovered, the money would be useful to—somebody.

So ran the *scenario*; but I fancy my juvenile pen hardly held on to the climax. My brief experience of boarding school occurred at this time, and I well remember writing "The Old Arm Chair" in a penny account book, in the schoolroom of Cresswell Lodge, and that I was both surprised and offended at the laughter of the kindly music-teacher who, coming into the room to summon a pupil, and seeing me gravely occupied, inquired what I was doing, and was intensely amused at my stolid method of composition, plodding on undisturbed by the voices and occupations of the older girls around me. "The Old Arm Chair" was certainly my first serious, painstaking effort in fiction; but as it was abandoned unfinished before my eleventh birthday, and as no line thereof ever achieved the distinction of type, it can hardly rank as my first novel.

There came a very few years later the sentimental period, in which my unfinished novels assumed a more ambitious form, and were modelled chiefly upon "Jane Eyre," with occasional tentative imitations of Thackeray. Stories of gentle hearts that loved in vain, always ending in renunciation. One romance there was, I well remember, begun with resolute purpose, after the first reading of "Esmond," and in the endeavour to give life and local colour to a story of the Restoration period, a brilliantly wicked interval in the social history of England, which, after the lapse of thirty years, I am still as bent upon taking for the background of a love story as I was when I began "Master

Anthony's Record" in Esmondese, and made my girlish acquaintance with the reading-room of the British Museum, where I went in quest of local colour, and where much kindness was shown to my youth and inexperience of the book world. Poring over a folio edition of the "State Trials" at my uncle's quiet rectory in sleepy Sandwich, I had discovered the passionate romantic story of Lord Grey's elopement with his sister-in-law, next in sequence to the trial of Lawrence Braddon and Hugh Speke for conspiracy. At the risk of seeming disloyal to my own race, I must add that it seemed to me a very tinpot order of plot to which these two learned gentlemen bent their legal minds, and which cost the Braddon family a heavy fine in land near Camelford—confiscation which I have heard my father complain of as especially unfair—Lawrence being a younger son. The romantic story of Lord Grey was to be the subject of "Master Anthony's Record," but Master Anthony's sentimental autobiography went the way of all my earlier efforts. It was but a year or so after the collapse of Master Anthony, that a blindly enterprising printer of Beverley, who had seen my poor little verses in the *Beverley Recorder*, made me the spirited offer of ten pounds for a serial story, to be set up and printed at Beverley, and published on commission by a London firm in Warwick Lane. I cannot picture to myself, in my after-knowledge of the bookselling trade, any enterprise more futile in its inception or more feeble in its execution; but to my youthful ambition the actual commission to write a novel, with an advance payment of fifty shillings to show good faith on the part of my Yorkshire speculator, seemed like the opening of that pen-and-ink paradise which I had sighed forever since I could hold a pen. I had, previously to this date, found a Mæcenas in Beverley, in the person of a learned gentleman who volunteered to foster my love of the Muses by buying the copyright of a volume of poems and publishing the same at his own expense—which he did, poor man, without stint, and by which noble patronage of Poet's Corner verse he must have lost money. He had, however, the privilege of dictating the subject of the principal poem, which was to sing—however feebly—Garibaldi's Sicilian campaign.

The Beverley printer suggested that my Warwick Lane serial should combine, as far as my powers allowed, the human interest and genial humour of Dickens with the plot-weaving of G. W. R. Reynolds; and, furnished with these broad instructions, I filled my ink-bottle, spread out my foolscap, and, on a hopelessly wet afternoon, began my first novel—now known as "The Trail of the Serpent"—but published in

Warwick Lane, and later in the stirring High Street of Beverley, as "Three Times Dead." In "Three Times Dead" I gave loose to all my leanings to the violent in melodrama. Death stalked in ghastliest form across my pages: and villainy reigned triumphant till the Nemesis of the last chapter. I wrote with all the freedom of one who feared not the face of a critic; and, indeed, thanks to the obscurity of its original production, and its re-issue as the ordinary two-shilling railway novel, this first novel of mine has almost entirely escaped the critical lash, and has pursued its way as a chartered libertine. People buy it and read it, and its faults and follies are forgiven as the exuberances of a pen unchastened by experience; but faster and more facile at that initial stage than it ever became after long practice.

I dashed headlong at my work, conjured up my images of horror or of mirth, and boldly built the framework of my story, and set my puppets moving. To me, at least, they were living creatures, who seemed to follow impulses of their own, to be impelled by their own passions, to love and hate, and plot and scheme of their own accord. There was unalloyed pleasure in the composition of that first story, and in the knowledge that it was to be actually printed and published, and not to be declined with thanks by adamantine magazine editors, like a certain short story which I had lately written, and which contained the germ of "Lady Audley's Secret." Indeed, at this period of my life, the postman's knock had become associated in my mind with the sharp sound of a rejected MS. dropping through the open letter-box on to the floor of the hall, while my heart seemed to drop in sympathy with that book-post packet.

Short of never being printed at all, my Beverley-born novel could have hardly entered upon the world of books in a more profound obscurity. That one living creature ever bought a number of "Three Times Dead" I greatly doubt. I can recall the thrill of emotion with which I tore open the envelope that contained my complimentary copy of the first number, folded across, and in aspect inferior to a gratis pamphlet about a patent medicine. The miserable little wood block which illustrated that first number would have disgraced a baker's whitey-brown bag, would have been unworthy to illustrate a penny bun. My spirits were certainly dashed at the technical shortcomings of that first serial, and I was hardly surprised when I was informed a few weeks later, that although my admirers at Beverley were deeply interested in the story, it was not a financial success, and that it would be only obliging on my part, and in accordance with my known kindness of heart, if I were to restrict the development of the romance to half its intended length, and to accept five pounds in lieu of ten as my reward. Having no desire that the rash Beverley printer should squander his own or his children's fortune in the obscurity of Warwick Lane, I immediately acceded to his request, shortened sail, and went on with my story, perhaps with a shade less enthusiasm, having seen the shabby figure it was to make in the book world. I may add that the Beverley publisher's payments began and ended with his noble advance of fifty shillings. The balance was never paid; and it was rather hard lines that, on his becoming bankrupt in his poor little way a few years later, a judge in the Bankruptcy Court remarked that, as Miss Braddon was now making a good deal of money by her pen, she ought to "come to the relief" of her first publisher.

And now my volume of verses being well under way, I went with my mother to farmhouse lodgings in the neighbourhood of that very Beverley, where I spent perhaps the happiest half-year of my life—half a year of tranquil, studious days, far from the madding crowd, with the mother whose society was always all sufficient for me—half a year among level pastures, with unlimited books from the library in Hull, an old farm-horse to ride about the green lanes, the breath of summer, with all its sweet odours of flower and herb, around and about us; half a year of unalloyed bliss, had it not been for one dark shadow, the heroic figure of Garibaldi, the sailor-soldier, looming large upon the foreground of my literary labours, as the hero of a lengthy narrative poem in the Spenserian metre.

My chief business at Beverley was to complete the volume of verse commissioned by my Yorkshire Mæcenas, at that time a very rich man, who paid me a much better price for my literary work than his townsman, the enterprising printer, and who had the first claim on my thought and time.

With the business-like punctuality of a salaried clerk, I went every morning to my file of the *Times*, and pored and puzzled over Neapolitan revolution and Sicilian campaign, and I can only say that if Emile Zola has suffered as much over Sedan as I suffered in the freshness of my youth, when flowery meadows and the old chestnut mare invited to summer idlesse, over the fighting in Sicily, his dogged perseverance in uncongenial labour should place him among the Immortal Forty. How I hated the great Joseph G. and the Spenserian metre, with its exacting demands upon the rhyming faculty! How I hated my own ignorance of modern Italian history, and my own eyes for never having looked upon Italian landscape, whereby historical allusion and local colour were both wanting to that dry-as-dust record of heroic endeavour! I had only the *Times* correspondent; where he was picturesque I could be picturesque—allowing always for the Spenserian straining—where he was rich in local colour I did my utmost to reproduce his colouring, stretched always on the Spenserian rack, and lengthened out by the bitter necessity of finding triple rhymes. Next to Giuseppe Garibaldi I hated Edmund Spenser, and it may be from a vengeful remembrance of those early struggles with a difficult form of versification, that, although throughout my literary life I have been a lover of England's earlier poets, and have delighted in the quaintness and *naïveté* of Chaucer, I have refrained from reading more than a casual stanza or two of the "Faëry Queen." When I lived at Beverley, Spenser was to me but a name, and Byron's "Childe Harold" was my only model for that exacting verse. I should add that the Beverley Mæcenas, when commissioning this volume of verse, was less superb in his ideas than the literary patron of the past. He looked at the matter from a purely commercial standpoint, and believed that a volume of verse, such as I could produce, would pay—a delusion on his part which I honestly strove to combat before accepting his handsome offer of remuneration for my time and labour. It was with this idea in his mind that he chose and insisted upon the Sicilian campaign as a subject for my muse, and thus started me heavily handicapped on the racecourse of Parnassus.

The weekly number of "Three Times Dead" was "thrown off" in brief intervals of rest from my *magnum opus*, and it was an infinite relief to turn from Garibaldi and his brothers in arms to the angels and the monsters which my own brain had engendered, and which to me seemed more alive than the good great man whose arms I so laboriously sang. My rustic pipe far better loved to sing of melodramatic poisoners and ubiquitous detectives; of fine houses in the West of London, and dark dens in the East. So the weekly chapter of my first novel ran merrily off my pen while the printer's boy waited in the farmhouse kitchen.

Happy, happy days, so near to memory, and yet so far! In that peaceful summer I finished my first novel, knocked Garibaldi on the head with a closing rhapsody, saw the York spring and summer races in hopelessly wet weather, learnt to love the Yorkshire people, and left Yorkshire almost broken-heartedly on a dull, grey October morning, to travel Londonwards through a landscape that was mostly under water.

And, behold, since that October morning I have written fifty-three novels; I have lost dear old friends and found new friends, who are also dear, but I have never looked on a Yorkshire landscape since I turned my reluctant eyes from those level meadows and green lanes where the old chestnut mare used to carry me ploddingly to and fro between tall, tangled hedges of eglantine and honeysuckle.

"The House of Elmore"

By F. W. Robinson

It is a far cry back to 1853, when dreams of writing a book had almost reached the boundary line of "probable events." I was then a pale, long-haired, consumptive-looking youth, who had been successful in prize poems—for there were prize competitions even in those far-off days—and in acrostics, and in the acceptance of one or two short stories, which had been actually published in a magazine that did not pay for contributions (it was edited by a clergyman of the Church of England, and the chaplain to a real duke), which magazine has gone the way of many magazines, and is now as extinct as the dodo. It was in the year 1853, or a month or two earlier, that I wrote my first novel—which, upon a moderate computation, I think, would make four or five good-sized library volumes, but I have never attempted to "scale" the manuscript. It is in my possession still, although I have not seen it for many weary years. It is buried with a heap more rubbish in a respectable old oak chest, the key of which is even lost to me. And yet that MS. was the turning-point of my small literary career. And it is the history of that manuscript which leads up to the publication of my first novel; my first step, though I did not know it, and hence it is part and parcel of the history of my first book—a link in the chain.

When that manuscript was completed, it was read aloud, night after night, to an admiring audience of family members, and pronounced as fit for publication as anything of Dickens or Thackeray or Bulwer, who were then in the full swing of their mighty capacities. Alas! I was a better judge than my partial and amiable critics. I had very grave doubts— "qualms," I think they are called—and I had read that it was uphill work to get a book published, and swagger through the world as a real live being who had actually written a novel. There was a faint hope, that was all; and so, with my MS. under my arm, I strolled into the palatial premises of Messrs. Hurst & Blackett ("successors to Henry Colburn" they proudly designated themselves at that period), laid my heavy parcel on the counter, and waited, with fear and trembling, for someone to emerge from the galleries of books and rows of desks beyond, and inquire the nature of my business. And here ensued my first surprise—quite a dramatic coincidence—for the tall, spare, middle-aged gentleman who advanced from the shadows towards the counter, proved, to my intense astonishment, to be a constant chess antagonist of mine at Kling's Chess Rooms, round the corner, in New Oxford Street—rooms which have long since disappeared, together with Horwitz, Harrwitz, Loewenthal, Williams, and other great chess lights of those far-away times, who were to be seen there, night after night, prepared for all comers. Kling's was a great chess house, and I was a chess enthusiast, as well as a youth who wanted to get into print. Failing literature, I had made up my mind to become a chess champion, if possible, although I knew already by quiet observation of my antagonists, that in that way madness lay, sheer uncontrollable, raging madness—for me at any rate. And the grave, middle-aged gentleman behind the counter of 13 Great Marlborough Street, proved to be the cashier of the firm, and used—being chess-mad with the rest of us—to spend his evenings at "Kling's." He was a player of my own strength, and for twelve months or so had I skirmished with him over the chessboard, and fought innumerable battles with him. He had never spoken of his occupation, nor I of my restless ambitions— chess players never go far beyond the chequered board.

"Hallo, Robinson!" he exclaimed in his surprise, "you don't mean to say that you—"

And then he stopped and regarded my youthful appearance very critically.

"Yes, Mr. Kenny—it's a novel," I said modestly; "my first."

"There's plenty of it," he remarked dryly. "I'll send it upstairs at once. And I'll wish you luck, too; but," he added, kindly preparing to soften the shock of a future refusal, "we have plenty of these come in—about seven a day—and most of them go back to their writers again."

"Ye-es, I suppose so," I answered, with a sigh.

For a while, however, I regarded the meeting as a happy augury—a lucky coincidence. I even had the vain, hopeless notion that Mr. Kenny might put in a good word for me, ask for special consideration, out of that kindly feeling which we had for each other, and which chess antagonists have invariably for each other, I am inclined to believe. But though we met three or four times a week, from that day forth not one word concerning the fate of my manuscript escaped the lips of Mr. Kenny. It is probable the incident had passed from his memory; he had nothing to do with the novel department itself, and the delivery of MSS. was a very common everyday proceeding to him. I was too bashful, perhaps too proud, an individual to ask any questions; but every evening that I encountered him I used to wonder "if he had heard anything," if any news of the book's fate had reached him, directly or indirectly; occasionally even, as time went on, I was disposed to imagine that he was letting me win the game out of kindness—for he was a gentle, kindly soul always—in order to soften the shock of a disappointment which he knew perfectly well was on its way towards me.

Some months afterwards, the fateful letter came to me from the firm, regretting its inability to make use of the MS., and expressing many thanks for a perusal of the same—a polite, concise, all-round kind of epistle, which a publisher is compelled to keep in stock, and to send out when rejected literature pours forth like a waterfall from the dusky caverns of a publishing house in a large way of business. It was all over, then—I had failed! From that hour I would turn chess player, and soften my brain in a quest for silver cups or champion amateur stakes. I could play chess better than I could write fiction, I was sure. Still, after some days of dead despair, I sent the MS. once more on its travels— this time to Smith & Elder's, whose reader, Mr. Williams, had leapt into singular prominence since his favourable judgment of Charlotte Brontë's book, and to whom most MSS. flowed spontaneously for many years afterwards. And in due course of time, Mr. Williams, acting for Messrs. Smith & Elder, asked me to call upon him—*for the MS.!*—at Cornhill, and there I received my first advice, my first thrill of exultation. "Presently, and probably, *and with perseverance*," he said, "you will succeed in literature, and if you will remember now, that to write a good novel is a very considerable achievement. Years of short story-writing is the best apprenticeship for you. Write and rewrite, and spare no pains." I thanked him, and I went home with tears in my eyes of gratitude and consolation, though my big story had been declined with thanks. But I did not write again. I put away my MS., and went on for six or eight hours a day at chess for many idle months before I was in the vein for composition, and then, with a sudden dash, I began "The House of Elmore." It was half finished when another strange incident occurred. I received one morning a letter from Lascelles Wraxall (afterwards Sir Lascelles Wraxall, Bart., as the reader may be probably aware), informing me that he was one of the readers for Messrs. Hurst & Blackett, and that it had been his duty sometime ago to decide unfavourably against a story which I had submitted to the notice of his firm, but that he had intended to write to me a private note urging me to adopt literature as a profession. His principal object in writing at that time was to suggest my trying the fortunes of the novel, which he had already read, with Messrs. Routledge, and he kindly added a letter of introduction to that firm in the Broadway—an introduction which, by the way, never came to anything.

Poor Lascelles Wraxall, clever writer and editor, press-man and literary adviser, real Bohemian and true friend—indeed, everybody's friend but his own—I look back at him with feelings of deep gratitude. He was a rolling stone, and when I met him for the first time in my life, years afterwards, he had left Marlborough Street for the Crimea; he had been given a commission in the Turkish Contingent at Kertch; he had come back anathematising the Service, and "chock full" of grievances against the Government, and he became once more editor and sub-editor, and publisher's hack even, until he stepped into his baronetcy—an empty title, for he had sold the reversion of the estates for a mere song long ago—and became special correspondent in Austria for the *Daily Telegraph*. And in Vienna he died, young in years still—not forty, I think—closing a life that only wanted one turn more of "application," I have often thought, to have achieved very great distinction. There are still a few writing men about who remember Lascelles Wraxall, but they are "the boys of the old brigade."

It was to Lascelles Wraxall I sent, when finished, "The House of Elmore," as the reader may very easily guess. Wraxall had stepped so much out of his groove—for the busy literary man that he was—to take me by the hand, and point the way along "the perilous road"; he had given me so many kind words, that I wrote my hardest to complete my new story before I should fade from his recollection. The book was finished in five weeks, and in hot haste, and for months again I was left wondering what the outcome of it all was to be; whether Wraxall was reading my story, or whether—oh, horror!—someother reader less kindly disposed, and more austere and critical, and hard to please, had been told off to sit in judgment upon my second MS.

I went back to chess for a distraction till the fate of that book was pronounced or sealed—it was always chess in the hours of my distress and anxiety—and I once again faced Charles Kenny, and once again wondered if he knew, and how much he knew, whilst he was deep in his king's gambit or his giuoco piano; but he was not even aware that I had sent in a second story, I learned afterwards. And then at last came the judgment—the pleasant, if formal, notice from Marlborough Street that the novel had been favourably reported upon by the reader, and that

Messrs. Hurst & Blackett would be pleased to see me at Marlborough Street to talk the matter of its publication over with me. Ah! what a letter that was!—what a surprise, after all!—what a good omen!

And some three months afterwards, at the end of the year 1854, my first book—but my second novel—was launched into the reading world, and I have hardly got over the feeling yet that I had actually a right to dub myself a novelist!

When the first three notices of the book appeared, wild dreams of a brilliant future beset me. They were all favourable notices—too favourable; but *John Bull*, *The Press*, and *Bell's Messenger* (I think they were the papers) scattered favourable notices indiscriminately at that time. Presently the *Athenæum* sobered me a little, but wound up with a kindly pat on the back, and the *Saturday Review*, then in its seventh number, drenched me with vitriolic acid, and brought me to a lower level altogether; and, finally, the *Morning Herald* blew a loud blast to my praise and glory—that last notice, I believe, having been written by my old friend Sir Edward Clarke, then a very young reviewer on the *Herald* staff, with no dreams of becoming Her Majesty's Solicitor-General just then! "The House of Elmore" actually paid its publishers' expenses, and left a balance, and brought me in a little cheque; and thus my writing life began in sober earnest.

"Dawn"

By H. Rider Haggard

I think that it was in an article by a fellow-scribe, where, doubtless more in sorrow than in anger, that gentleman exposed the worthlessness of the productions of sundry of his brother authors, in which I read that whatever success I had met with as a writer of fiction was due to my literary friends and "nepotic criticism." This is scarcely the case, since when I began to write I do not think that I knew a single creature who had published books—blue books alone excepted. Nobody was ever more outside the ring, or less acquainted with the art of "rolling logs," than the humble individual who pens these lines. But the reader shall judge for himself.

To begin at the beginning: My very first attempt at imaginative writing was made while I was a boy at school. One of the masters promised a prize to that youth who should best describe on paper any incident, real or imaginary. I entered the lists, and selected the scene at an operation in a hospital as my subject. The fact that I had never seen an operation, nor crossed the doors of a hospital, did not deter me from this bold endeavour, which, however, was justified by its success. I was declared to have won in the competition, though, probably through the forgetfulness of the master, I remember that I never received the promised prize. My next literary effort, written in 1876, was an account of a Zulu war dance, which I witnessed when I was on the staff of the Governor of Natal. It was published in the *Gentleman's Magazine*, and very kindly noticed in various papers. A year later I wrote another article, entitled "A Visit to the Chief Secocoeni," which very nearly got me into trouble. I was then serving on the staff of Sir Theophilus Shepstone, and the article, signed with my initials, reached South Africa in its printed form shortly after the annexation of the Transvaal. Young men with a pen in their hands are proverbially indiscreet, and in this instance I was no exception. In the course of my article I had described the Transvaal Boer at home with a fidelity that should be avoided by members of a diplomatic mission, and had even gone the length of saying that most of the Dutch women were "fat." Needless to say, my remarks were translated into the Africander papers, and somewhat extensively read, especially by the ladies in question and their male relatives; nor did the editors of those papers forbear to comment on them in leading articles. Shortly afterwards, there was a great and stormy meeting of Boers at Pretoria. As matters began to look serious, somebody ventured among them to ascertain the exciting cause, and returned with the pleasing intelligence that they were all talking of what the Englishman had written about the physical proportions of their womenkind and domestic habits, and threatening to take up arms to avenge it. Of my feelings on learning this news I will not discourse, but they were uncomfortable, to say the least of it. Happily, in the end, the gathering broke up without bloodshed, but when the late Sir Bartle Frere came to Pretoria, some months afterwards, he administered to me a sound and well-deserved lecture on my indiscretion. I excused myself by saying that I had set down nothing which was not strictly true, and he replied to the effect that therein lay my fault. I quite agree with him; indeed, there is little doubt but that these bald statements of fact as to the stoutness of the Transvaal "fraus," and the lack of cleanliness in their homes, went near to precipitating a result that, as it chanced, was postponed for several years. Well, it is all done with now, and I take this opportunity of apologising to such of the ladies in question as may still be in the land of life.

This unfortunate experience cooled my literary ardour, yet, as it chanced, when some five years later I again took up my pen, it was in connection with African affairs. These pages are no place for politics, but I must allude to them in explanation. It will be remembered that the Transvaal was annexed by Great Britain in 1877. In 1881 the Boers rose in rebellion and administered several thrashings to our troops, whereon the Government of this country came suddenly to the conclusion that a wrong had been done to the victors, and, subject to some paper restrictions, gave them back their independence. As it chanced, at the time I was living on some African property belonging to me in the centre of the operations, and so disgusted was I, in common with thousands of others, at the turn which matters had taken, that I shook the dust of South Africa off my feet and returned to England. Now, the first impulse of an aggrieved Englishman is to write to the *Times*, and if I remember right I took this course, but, my letter not being inserted, I enlarged upon the idea and composed a book called "Cetewayo and his White Neighbours." This semi-political work, or rather history, was very carefully constructed from the records of some six years' experience, and by the help of a shelf full of blue books that stare me in the face as I write these words; and the fact that it still goes on selling seems to show that it has some value in the eyes of students of South African politics. But when I had written my book I was confronted by a difficulty which I had not anticipated, being utterly without experience in such affairs—that of finding somebody willing to publish it. I remember that I purchased a copy of the *Athenæum*, and selecting the names of various firms at hazard, wrote to them offering to submit my manuscript, but, strange to say, none of them seemed anxious to peruse it. At last—how I do not recollect—it came into the hands of Messrs. Trübner, who, after consideration, wrote to say that they were willing to bring it out on the half profit system, provided that I paid down fifty pounds towards the cost of production. I did not at all like the idea of parting with the fifty pounds, but I believed in my book, and was anxious to put my views on the Transvaal rebellion and other African questions before the world. So I consented to the terms, and in due course "Cetewayo" was published in a neat green binding. Somewhat to my astonishment, it proved a success from a literary point of view. It was not largely purchased—indeed, that fifty pounds took several years on its return journey to my pocket, but it was favourably, and in some instances almost enthusiastically, reviewed, especially in the colonial papers.

About this time the face of a girl whom I saw in a church at Norwood gave me the idea of writing a novel. The face was so perfectly beautiful, and at the same time so refined, that I felt I could fit a story to it which should be worthy of a heroine similarly endowed. When next I saw Mr. Trübner I consulted him on the subject.

"You can write—it is certain that you can write. Yes, do it, and I will get the book published for you," he answered.

Thus encouraged I set to work. How to compose a novel I knew not, so I wrote straight on, trusting to the light of nature to guide me. My main object was to produce the picture of a woman perfect in mind and body, and to show her character ripening and growing spiritual, under the pressure of various afflictions. Of course, there is a vast gulf between a novice's aspiration and his attainment, and I do not contend that Angela as she appears in "Dawn" fulfils this ideal; also, such a person in real life might, and probably would, be a bore—

> *Something too bright and good*
> *For human nature's daily food.*

Still, this was the end I aimed at. Indeed, before I had done with her, I became so deeply attached to my heroine that, in a literary sense, I have never quite got over it. I worked very hard at this novel during the next six months or so, but at length it was finished and despatched to Mr. Trübner, who, as his firm did not deal in this class of book, submitted it to five or six of the best publishers of fiction. One and all they declined it, so that by degrees it became clear to me that I might as well have saved my labour. Mr. Trübner, however, had confidence in my work, and submitted the manuscript to Mr. John Cordy Jeaffreson for report; and here I may pause to say that I think there is more kindness in the hearts of literary men than is common in the world. It is not a pleasant task, in the face of repeated failure, again and again to attempt the adventure of persuading brother publishers to undertake the maiden effort of an unknown man. Still less pleasant is it, as I can vouch from experience, to wade through a lengthy and not particularly legible manuscript, and write an elaborate opinion thereon for the benefit of a stranger. Yet Mr. Trübner and Mr. Jeaffreson did these things for me without fee or reward. Mr. Jeaffreson's report I have lost or mislaid, but I remember its purport well. It was to the effect that there was a great deal of power in the novel, but that it required to be entirely rewritten. The first part he thought so good that he advised me to expand it, and the unhappy ending he could not agree with. If I killed the heroine, it would kill the book, he said. He may have been right, but I still hold to my first conception, according to which Angela was doomed to an early and pathetic end, as the fittest crown to her career. That the story needed rewriting there is no doubt, but I believe that it would have been better as a work of art if I had dealt with it on the old lines, especially as the expansion of the beginning, in accordance with the advice of my kindly critic, took the tale back through the history of another generation—always a most dangerous experiment. Still, I did as I was told, not presuming to set up a judgment of my own in the matter. If I had worked hard at the first draft of the novel, I worked much harder at the second, especially as I could not give all my leisure to it, being engaged at the time in reading for the Bar. So hard did I work that at length my eyesight gave out, and I was obliged to complete the last hundred sheets in a darkened room. But let my eyes ache as they might, I would not give up till it was finished, within about three months from the date of its commencement. Recently, I went through this book to prepare it for a new edition, chiefly in order to cut out some of the mysticism and tall writing, for which it is too remarkable, and was pleased to find that it still interested me. But if a writer may be allowed to criticise his own work, it is two books, not one. Also, the hero is a very poor creature. Evidently I was too much occupied with my heroines to give much thought to him; moreover, women are so much easier and more interesting to write about, for whereas no two of them are alike, in modern men, or rather, in young men of the middle and upper classes, there is a paralysing sameness. As a candid friend once said to me, "There is nothing manly about that chap, Arthur"— he is the hero—"except his bull-dog!" With Angela herself I am still in love; only she ought to have died, which, on the whole, would have been a better fate than being married to Arthur, more especially if he was anything like the illustrator's conception of him in the current edition.

In its new shape "Dawn" was submitted to Messrs. Hurst & Blackett, and at once accepted by that firm. Why it was called "Dawn" I am not now quite clear, but I think it was because I could find no other title acceptable to the publishers. The discovery of suitable titles is a more difficult matter than people who do not write romances would suppose, most of the good ones having been used already and copyrighted. In due course the novel was published in three fat volumes, and a pretty green cover, and I sat down to await events. At the best I did not expect to win a fortune out of it, as if everyone of the five hundred copies printed were sold, I could only make fifty pounds under my agreement—not an extravagant reward for a great deal of labour. As a matter of fact, but four hundred and fifty sold, so the net proceeds of the venture amounted to ten pounds only, and forty surplus copies of the book, which I bored my friends by presenting to them. But as the copyright of the work reverted to me at the expiration of a year, I cannot grumble at this result. The reader may think that it was mercenary of me to consider my first book from this financial point of view, but to be frank, though the story interested me much in its writing, and I had a sneaking belief in its merits, it never occurred to me that I, an utterly inexperienced beginner, could hope to make any mark in competition with the many brilliant writers of fiction who were already before the public. Therefore, so far as I was concerned, any reward in the way of literary reputation seemed to be beyond my reach.

It was on the occasion of the publication of this novel that I made my first and last attempt to "roll a log," with somewhat amusing results.

Almost the only person of influence whom I knew in the world of letters was the editor of a certain society paper. I had not seen him for ten years, but at this crisis I ventured to recall myself to his memory, and to ask him, not for a favourable notice, but that the book should be reviewed in his journal. He acceded to my prayer; it was reviewed, but after a fashion for which I did not bargain. This little incident taught me a lesson, and the moral of it is: never trouble an editor about your immortal works; he can so easily be even with you. I commend it to all literary tiros. Even if you are in a position to command "puffs," the public will find you out in the second edition, and revenge itself upon your next book. Here is a story that illustrates the accuracy of this statement; it came to me on good authority, and I believe it to be true. A good many years ago, the relation of an editor of a great paper published a novel. It was a bad novel, but a desperate effort was made to force it upon the public, and in many of the leading journals appeared notices so laudatory that readers fell into the trap, and the book went through several editions. Encouraged by success, the writer published a second book, but the public had found her out, and it fell flat. Being a person of resource, she brought out a third work under a *nom de plume*, which, as at first, was accorded an enthusiastic reception by previous arrangement, and forced into circulation. A fourth followed under the same name, but again the public had found her out, and her career as a novelist came to an end.

To return to the fate of "Dawn." In most quarters it met with the usual reception of a first novel by an unknown man. Some of the reviewers sneered at it, and some "slated" it, and made merry over the misprints—a cheap form of wit that saves those who practise it the trouble of going into the merits of a book. Two very good notices fell to its lot, however, in the *Times* and in the *Morning Post*, the first of these speaking about the novel in terms of which any amateur writer might feel proud, though, unfortunately, it appeared too late to be of much service. Also, I discovered that the story had interested a great many readers, and none of them more than the late Mr. Trübner, through whose kind offices it came to be published, who, I was told, paid me the strange compliment of continuing its perusal till within a few hours of his death, a sad event that the enemy might say was hastened thereby. In this connection I remember that the first hint I received that my story was popular with the ordinary reading public, whatever reviewers might say of it, came from the lips of a young lady, a chance visitor at my house, whose name

I have forgotten. Seeing the book lying on the table, she took a volume up, saying—

"Oh, have you read 'Dawn'? It is a first-rate novel; I have just finished it." Somebody explained, and the subject dropped, but I was not a little gratified by the unintended compliment.

These facts encouraged me, and I wrote a second novel—"The Witch's Head." This book I endeavoured to publish serially by posting the MS. to the editors of various magazines for their consideration. But in those days there were no literary agents or Authors' Societies to help young writers with their experience and advice, and the bulky manuscript always came back to my hand like a boomerang, till at length I wearied of the attempt. Of course I sent to the wrong people; afterwards the editor of a leading monthly told me that he would have been delighted to run the book had it fallen into the hands of his firm. In the end, as in the case of "Dawn," I published "The Witch's Head" in three volumes. Its reception astonished me, for I did not think so well of the book as I had done of its predecessor. In that view, by the way, the public has borne out my judgment, for to this day three copies of "Dawn" are absorbed for every two of "The Witch's Head," a proportion that has never varied since the two works appeared in one-volume form.

"The Witch's Head" was very well reviewed; indeed, in one or two cases, the notices were almost enthusiastic, most of all when they dealt with the African part of the book, which I had inserted as padding, the fight between Jeremy and the Boer giant being singled out for especial praise. Whatever it may lack, one merit this novel has, however, that was overlooked by all the reviewers. Omitting the fictitious incidents introduced for the purposes of the story, it contains an accurate account of the great disaster inflicted upon our troops by the Zulus at Isandhlwana. I was in the country at the time of the massacre, and heard its story from the lips of survivors; also, in writing of it, I studied the official reports in the blue books and the minutes of the court martial.

"The Witch's Head" attained the dignity of being pirated in America, and in England went out of print in a few weeks, but no argument that I could use would induce my publishers to re-issue it in a one volume edition. The risk was too great, they said. Then it was I came to the conclusion that I would abandon the making of books. The work was very hard, and when put to the test of experience the glamour that surrounds this occupation vanished. I did not care much for the publicity it involved, and, like most young authors, I failed to appreciate being sneered at by anonymous critics who happened not to admire what I wrote, and whom I had no opportunity of answering. It is true that then, as now, I liked the work for its own sake. Indeed, I have always thought that literature would be a charming profession if its conditions allowed of the depositing of manuscripts, when completed, in a drawer, there to language in obscurity, or of their private publication only. But I could not afford myself these luxuries. I was too modest to hope for any renown worth having, and for the rest the game seemed scarcely worth the candle. I had published a history and two novels. On the history I had lost fifty pounds, on the first novel I had made ten pounds, and on the second fifty; net profit on the three, ten pounds, which in the case of a man with other occupations and duties did not appear to be an adequate return for the labour involved. But I was not destined to escape thus from the toils of romance. One day I chanced to read a clever article in favour of boys' books, and it occurred to me that I might be able to do as well as others in that line. I was working at the Bar at the time, but in my spare evenings, more from amusement than from any other reason, I entered on the literary adventure that ended in the appearance of "King Solomon's Mines." This romance has proved very successful, although three firms, including my own publishers, refused even to consider it. But as it can scarcely be called one of my first books, I shall not speak of it here.

In conclusion, I will tell a moving tale, that it may be a warning to young authors forever. After my publishers declined to issue "The Witch's Head" in a six-shilling edition, I tried many others without success, and at length in my folly signed an agreement with a firm since deceased. Under this document the firm in question agreed to bring out "Dawn" and "The Witch's Head" in a two-shilling edition, and generously to remunerate me with a third share in the profits realised, if any. In return for this concession, I on my part undertook to allow the said firm to republish any novel that I might write, for a period of five years from the date of the agreement, in a two-shilling form, and on the same third-profit terms. Of course, so soon as the success of "King Solomon's Mines" was established, I received a polite letter from the publishers in question, asking when they might expect to republish that romance at two shillings. Then the matter came under the consideration of lawyers and other skilled persons, with the result that it appeared that, if the Courts took a strict view of the agreement, ruin stared me in the face, so far as my literary affairs were concerned. To begin with, either by accident or design, this artful document was so worded that, *primâ facie*, the contracting publisher had a right to place his cheap edition on the market whenever it might please him to do so, subject only to the payment of a third of the profit, to be assessed by himself, which practically might have meant nothing at all. How could I expect to dispose of work subject to such a legal "servitude"? For five long years I was a slave to the framer of the "hanging" clause of the agreement. Things looked black indeed, when, thanks to the diplomacy of my agent, and to a fortunate change in the *personnel* of the firm to which I was bound, I avoided disaster. The fatal agreement was cancelled, and in consideration of my release I undertook to write two books upon a moderate royalty. Thus, then, did I escape out of bondage. To be just, it was my own fault that I should ever have been sold into it, but authors are proverbially guileless when they are anxious to publish their books, and a piece of printed paper with a few additions written in a neat hand looks innocent enough. Now no such misfortunes need happen, for the Authors' Society is ready and anxious to protect them from themselves and others, but in those days it did not exist.

This is the history of how I drifted into the writing of books. If it saves one beginner so inexperienced and unfriended as I was in those days from putting his hand to a "hanging" agreement under any circumstances whatsoever, it will not have been set out in vain.

The advice that I give to would-be authors, if I may presume to offer it, is to think for a long while before they enter at all upon a career so hard and hazardous, but having entered on it, not to be easily cast down. There are great virtues in perseverance, even though critics sneer and publishers prove unkind.

"Hudson's Bay"

By R. M. Ballantyne

Having been asked to give some account of the commencement of my literary career, I begin by remarking that my first book was not a tale or "story-book," but a free-and-easy record of personal adventure and everyday life in those wild regions of North America which are known, variously, as Rupert's Land—The Hudson's Bay Territory—The Nor' West, and "The Great Lone Land."

The record was never meant to see the light in the form of a book. It was written solely for the eye of my mother, but, as it may be said that it was the means of leading me ultimately into the path of my life-work, and was penned under somewhat peculiar circumstances, it may not be out of place to refer to it particularly here.

The circumstances were as follows:—

After having spent about six years in the wild Nor' West, as a servant of the Hudson's Bay Fur Company, I found myself, one summer—at the advanced age of twenty-two—in charge of an outpost on the uninhabited northern shores of the Gulf of St. Lawrence named Seven Islands. It was a dreary, desolate spot; at that time far beyond the bounds of civilisation. The gulf, just opposite the establishment, was about fifty miles broad. The ships which passed up and down it were invisible, not only on account of distance, but because of seven islands at the mouth of the bay coming between them and the outpost. My next neighbour, in command of a similar post up the gulf, was about seventy miles distant. The nearest house down the gulf was about eighty miles off, and behind us lay the virgin forests, with swamps, lakes, prairies, and mountains, stretching away without break right across the continent to the Pacific Ocean.

The outpost—which, in virtue of a ship's carronade and a flagstaff, was occasionally styled a "fort"—consisted of four wooden buildings. One of these—the largest, with a verandah—was the Residency. There was an offshoot in rear which served as a kitchen. The other houses were a store for goods wherewith to carry on trade with the Indians, a stable, and a workshop. The whole population of the establishment—indeed of the surrounding district—consisted of myself and one man—also a horse! The horse occupied the stable, I dwelt in the Residency, the rest of the population lived in the kitchen.

There were, indeed, five other men belonging to the establishment, but these did not affect its desolation, for they were away netting salmon at a river about twenty miles distant at the time I write of.

My "Friday"—who was a French-Canadian—being cook, as well as man-of-all-works, found a little occupation in attending to the duties of his office, but the unfortunate Governor had nothing whatever to do except await the arrival of Indians, who were not due at that time. The horse was a bad one, without a saddle, and in possession of a pronounced backbone. My "Friday" was not sociable. I had no books, no newspapers, no magazines or literature of any kind, no game to shoot, no boat wherewith to prosecute fishing in the bay, and no prospect of seeing anyone to speak to for weeks, if not months, to come. But I had pen and ink, and, by great good fortune, was in possession of a blank paper book fully an inch thick.

These, then, were the circumstances in which I began my first book.

When that book was finished, and, not long afterwards, submitted to the—I need hardly say favourable—criticism of my mother, I had not the most distant idea of taking to authorship as a profession. Even when a printer-cousin, seeing the MS., offered to print it, and the well-known Blackwood of Edinburgh, seeing the book, offered to publish it—and did publish it—my ambition was still so absolutely asleep that I did not again put pen to paper in *that* way for eight years thereafter, although I might have been encouraged thereto by the fact that this first book—named "Hudson's Bay"—besides being a commercial success, received favourable notice from the Press.

It was not until the year 1854 that my literary path was opened up. At that time I was a partner in the late publishing firm of Constable & Co., of Edinburgh. Happening one day to meet with the late William Nelson, publisher, I was asked by him how I should like the idea of taking to literature as a profession. My answer I forget. It must have been vague, for I had never thought of the subject before.

"Well," said he, "what would you think of trying to write a story?"

Somewhat amused, I replied that I did not know what to think, but I would try if he wished me to do so.

"Do so," said he, "and go to work at once"—or words to that effect.

I went to work at once, and wrote my first story or work of fiction. It was published in 1855 under the name of "Snowflakes and Sunbeams; or, The Young Fur-traders." Afterwards the first part of the title was dropped, and the book is now known as "The Young Fur-traders." From that day to this I have lived by making story-books for young folk.

From what I have said it will be seen that I have never aimed at the achieving of this position, and I hope that it is not presumptuous in me to think—and to derive much comfort from the thought—that God led me into the particular path along which I have walked for so many years.

The scene of my first story was naturally laid in those backwoods with which I was familiar, and the story itself was founded on the adventures and experiences of myself and my companions. When a second book was required of me, I stuck to the same regions, but changed the locality. When casting about in my mind for a suitable subject, I happened to meet with an old retired "Nor'wester" who had spent an adventurous life in Rupert's Land. Among other duties he had been sent to establish an outpost of the Hudson's Bay Company at Ungava Bay, one of the most dreary parts of a desolate region. On hearing what I wanted he sat down and wrote a long narrative of his proceedings there, which he placed at my disposal, and thus furnished me with the foundation of "Ungava."

But now I had reached the end of my tether, and when a third story was wanted I was compelled to seek new fields of adventure in the books of travellers. Regarding the Southern seas as a most romantic part of the world—after the backwoods!—I mentally and spiritually plunged into those warm waters, and the dive resulted in the "Coral Island."

It now began to be borne in upon me that there was something not quite satisfactory in describing, expatiating on, and energising in, regions which one has never seen. For one thing, it was needful to be always carefully on the watch to avoid falling into mistakes—geographical, topographical, natural-historical, and otherwise.

For instance, despite the utmost care of which I was capable while studying up for the "Coral Island," I fell into a blunder through ignorance in regard to a familiar fruit. I was under the impression that cocoanuts grew on their trees in the same form as that in which they are usually presented to us in grocers' windows—namely, about the size of a large fist, with three spots at one end. Learning from trustworthy books that at a certain stage of development the nut contains a delicious beverage like lemonade, I sent one of my heroes up a tree for a nut, through the shell of which he bored a hole with a penknife. It was not till long after the story was published that my own brother—who had voyaged in Southern seas—wrote to draw my attention to the fact that the cocoanut is nearly as large as a man's head, and its outer husk is over an inch thick, so that no ordinary penknife could bore to its interior! Of course I should have known this, and, perhaps, should be ashamed of my ignorance, but, somehow I'm not!

I admit that this was a slip, but such, and other slips, hardly justify the remark that some people have not hesitated to make—namely, that I have a tendency to draw the long bow. I feel almost sensitive on this point, for I have always laboured to be true to nature and to fact even in my wildest flights of fancy.

This reminds me of the remark made to myself once by a lady in reference to this same "Coral Island." "There is one thing, Mr. Ballantyne," she said, "which I really find it hard to believe. You make one of your three boys dive into a clear pool, go to the bottom, and then, turning on his back, look up and wink and laugh at the other two."

"No, no, not '*laugh*,'" said I, remonstratively.

"Well, then, you make him smile."

"Ah! that is true, but there is a vast difference between laughing and smiling under water. But is it not singular that you should doubt the only incident in the story which I personally verify? I happened to be in lodgings at the seaside while writing that story, and, after penning the passage you refer to, I went down to the shore, pulled off my clothes, dived to the bottom, turned on my back, and, looking up, I smiled and winked."

The lady laughed, but I have never been quite sure, from the tone of that laugh, whether it was a laugh of conviction or of unbelief. It is not improbable that my fair friend's mental constitution may have been somewhat similar to that of the old woman who declined to believe her sailor-grandson when he told her he had seen flying-fish, but at once recognised his veracity when he said he had seen the remains of Pharaoh's chariot wheels on the shores of the Red Sea.

Recognising, then, the difficulties of my position, I formed the resolution to visit—when possible—the scenes in which my stories were laid; converse with the people who, under modification, were to form the *dramatis personæ* of the tales, and, generally, to obtain information in each case, as far as lay in my power, from the fountain-head.

Thus, when about to begin "The Lifeboat," I went to Ramsgate, and, for sometime, was hand and glove with Jarman, the heroic coxswain of the Ramsgate boat, a lion-like as well as a lion-hearted man, who rescued hundreds of lives from the fatal Goodwin Sands during his career. In like manner, when getting up information for "The Lighthouse," I obtained permission from the Commissioners of Northern Lights to visit the Bell Rock Lighthouse, where I hobnobbed with the three keepers of that celebrated pillar-in-the-sea for three weeks, and read Stevenson's graphic account of the building of the structure in the library, or visitors' room, just under the lantern. I was absolutely a prisoner there during those three weeks, for no boats ever came near us, and it need scarcely be said that ships kept well out of our way. By good fortune there came on a pretty stiff gale at the time, and Stevenson's thrilling narrative was read to the tune of whistling winds and roaring seas, many of which latter sent the spray right up to the lantern and caused the building, more than once, to quiver to its foundation.

In order to do justice to "Fighting the Flames" I careered through the streets of London on fire-engines, clad in a pea-jacket and a black leather helmet of the Salvage Corps. This to enable me to pass the cordon of police without question—though not without recognition, as was made apparent to me on one occasion at a fire by a fireman whispering confidentially, "I know what *you* are, sir, you're a hamitoor!"

"Right you are," said I, and moved away in order to change the subject.

It was a glorious experience, by the way, this galloping on fire-engines through the crowded streets. It had in it much of the excitement of the chase—possibly that of war—with the noble end in view of saving instead of destroying life! Such tearing along at headlong speed; such wild roaring of the firemen to clear the way; such frantic dashing aside of cabs, carts, 'buses, and pedestrians; such reckless courage on the part of the men, and volcanic spoutings on the part of the fires! But I must not linger. The memory of it is too enticing. "Deep Down" took me to Cornwall, where, over two hundred fathoms beneath the green turf, and more than half a mile out under the bed of the sea, I saw the sturdy miners at work winning copper and tin from the solid rock, and acquired some knowledge of their life, sufferings, and toils.

In the land of the Vikings I shot ptarmigan, caught salmon, and gathered material for "Erling the Bold." A winter in Algiers made me familiar with the "Pirate City." I enjoyed a fortnight with the hearty inhabitants of the Gull Lightship off the Goodwin Sands; and went to the Cape of Good Hope and up into the interior of the Colony, to spy out the land and hold intercourse with "The Settler and the Savage"—

although I am bound to confess that, with regard to the latter, I talked to him only with mine eyes. I also went afloat for a short time with the fishermen of the North Sea in order to be able to do justice to "The Young Trawler."

To arrive still closer at the truth, and to avoid errors, I have always endeavoured to submit my proof sheets, when possible, to experts and men who knew the subjects well. Thus, Captain Shaw, late chief of the London Fire Brigade, kindly read the proofs of "Fighting the Flames," and prevented my getting off the rails in matters of detail, and Sir Arthur Blackwood, financial secretary to the General Post Office, obligingly did me the same favour in regard to "Post Haste."

One other word in conclusion. Always, while writing—whatever might be the subject of my story—I have been influenced by an undercurrent of effort and desire to direct the minds and affections of my readers towards the higher life.

"The Premier and the Painter"

By I. Zangwill

As it is scarcely two years since my name (which, I hear, is a *nom de plume*) appeared in print on the cover of a book, I may be suspected of professional humour when I say I do not really know which was my first book. Yet such is the fact. My literary career has been so queer that I find it not easy to write my autobibliography.

"What is a pound?" asked Sir Robert Peel in an interrogative mood futile as Pilate's. "What is a book?" I ask, and the dictionary answers with its usual dogmatic air, "A collection of sheets of paper, or similar material, blank, written, or printed, bound together." At this rate my first book would be that romance of school life in two volumes, which, written in a couple of exercise books, circulated gratuitously in the schoolroom, and pleased our youthful imaginations with teacher-baiting tricks we had not the pluck to carry out in the actual. I shall always remember this story because, after making the tour of the class, it was returned to me with thanks and a new first page from which all my graces of style had evaporated. Indignant inquiry discovered the criminal—he admitted he had lost the page, and had rewritten it from memory. He pleaded that it was better written (which in one sense was true), and that none of the facts had been omitted.

This ill-treated tale was "published" when I was ten, but an old schoolfellow recently wrote to me reminding me of an earlier novel written in an old account-book. Of this I have no recollection, but, as he says he wrote it day by day at my dictation, I suppose he ought to know. I am glad to find I had so early achieved the distinction of keeping an amanuensis.

The dignity of print I achieved not much later, contributing verses and virtuous essays to various juvenile organs. But it was not till I was eighteen that I achieved a printed first book. The story of this first book is peculiar; and, to tell it in approved story form, I must request the reader to come back two years with me.

One fine day, when I was sixteen, I was wandering about the Ramsgate sands looking for Toole. I did not really expect to see him, and I had no reason to believe he was in Ramsgate, but I thought if Providence were kind to him it might throw him in my way. I wanted to do him a good turn. I had written a three-act farcical comedy at the request of an amateur dramatic club. I had written out all the parts, and I think there were rehearsals. But the play was never produced. In the light of after knowledge I suspect some of those actors must have been of quite professional calibre. You understand, therefore, why my thoughts turned to Toole. But I could not find Toole. Instead, I found on the sands a page of a paper called *Society*. It is still running merrily at a penny, but at that time it had also a Saturday edition at threepence. On this page was a great prize-competition scheme, as well as details of a regular weekly competition. The competitions in those days were always literary and intellectual, but then popular education had not made such strides as today.

I sat down on the spot, and wrote something which took a prize in the weekly competition. This emboldened me to enter for the great stakes.

There were various events. I resolved to enter for two. One was a short novel, and the other a comedietta. The "5*l.* humorous story" competition I did not go in for; but when the last day of sending in MSS. for that had passed, I reproached myself with not having despatched one of my manuscripts. Modesty had prevented me sending in old work, as I felt assured it would stand no chance, but when it was too late I was annoyed with myself for having thrown away a possibility. After all I could have lost nothing. Then I discovered that I had mistaken the last date, and that there was still a day. In the joyful reaction I selected a story called "Professor Grimmer," and sent it in. Judge of my amazement when this got the prize (5*l.*), and was published in serial form running through three numbers of *Society*. Last year, at a Press dinner, I found myself next to Mr. Arthur Goddard, who told me he had acted as Competition Editor, and that quite a number of now well-known people had taken part in these admirable competitions. My painfully laboured novel only got honourable mention, and my comedietta was lost in the post.

But I was now at the height of literary fame, and success stimulated me to fresh work. I still marvel when I think of the amount of rubbish I turned out in my seventeenth and eighteenth years, in the scanty leisure of a harassed pupil-teacher at an elementary school, working hard in the evenings for a degree at the London University to boot. There was a fellow pupil-teacher (let us call him Y.) who believed in me, and who had a little money with which to back his belief. I was for starting a comic paper. The name was to be *Grimaldi*, and I was to write it all every week.

"But don't you think your invention would give way ultimately?" asked Y. It was the only time he ever doubted me.

"By that time I shall be able to afford a staff," I replied triumphantly.

Y. was convinced. But before the comic paper was born, Y. had another happy thought. He suggested that if I wrote a Jewish story, we might make enough to finance the comic paper. I was quite willing. If he had suggested an epic, I should have written it.

So I wrote the story in four evenings (I always write in spurts), and within ten days from the inception of the idea the booklet was on sale in a coverless pamphlet form. The printing cost ten pounds. I paid five (the five I had won), Y. paid five, and we divided the profits. He has since not become a publisher.

My first book (price one penny nett) went well. It was loudly denounced by those it described, and widely bought by them; it was hawked about the streets. One little shop in Whitechapel sold 400 copies. It was even on Smith's bookstalls. There was great curiosity among Jews to know the name of the writer. Owing to my anonymity, I was enabled to see those enjoying its perusal, who were afterwards to explain to me their horror and disgust at its illiteracy and vulgarity. By vulgarity vulgar Jews mean the reproduction of the Hebrew words with which the poor and the old-fashioned interlard their conversation. It is as if English-speaking Scotchmen and Irishmen should object to "dialect" novels reproducing the idiom of their "uncultured" countrymen. I do not possess a copy of my first book, but somehow or other I discovered the MS. when writing "Children of the Ghetto." The description of market-day in Jewry was transferred bodily from the MS. of my first book, and is now generally admired.

What the profits were I never knew, for they were invested in the second of our publications. Still jealously keeping the authorship secret, we published a long comic ballad which I had written on the model of "Bab." With this we determined to launch out in style, and so we had gorgeous advertisement posters printed in three colours, which were to be stuck about London to beautify that great dreary city. Y. saw the black-hair of Fortune almost within our grasp.

One morning our headmaster walked into my room with a portentously solemn air. I felt instinctively that the murder was out. But he only said, "Where is Y.?" though the mere coupling of our names was ominous, for our publishing partnership was unknown. I replied, "How should I know? In his room, I suppose."

He gave me a peculiar sceptical glance.

"When did you last see Y.?" he said.

"Yesterday afternoon," I replied wonderingly.

"And you don't know where he is now?"

"Haven't an idea—isn't he in school?"

"No," he replied in low, awful tones.

"Where then?" I murmured.

"*In prison!*"

"In prison!" I gasped.

"In prison; I have just been to help bail him out."

It transpired that Y. had suddenly been taken with a further happy thought. Contemplation of those gorgeous tricoloured posters had turned his brain, and, armed with an amateur paste-pot and a ladder, he had sallied forth at midnight to stick them about the silent streets, so as to cut down the publishing expenses. A policeman, observing him at work, had told him to get down, and Y., being legal-minded, had argued it out with the policeman *de haut en bas* from the top of his ladder. The outraged majesty of the law thereupon haled Y. off to the cells.

Naturally the cat was now out of the bag, and the fat in the fire.

To explain away the poster was beyond the ingenuity of even a professed fiction-monger.

Straightway the committee of the school was summoned in hot haste, and held debate upon the scandal of a pupil-teacher being guilty of originality. And one dread afternoon, when all Nature seemed to hold its breath, I was called down to interview a member of the committee. In his hand were copies of the obnoxious publications.

I approached the great person with beating heart. He had been kind to me in the past, singling me out, on account of some scholastic successes, for an annual vacation at the seaside. It has only just struck me, after all these years, that, if he had not done so, I should not have found the page of *Society*, and so not have perpetrated the deplorable compositions.

In the course of a bad quarter of an hour, he told me that the ballad was tolerable, though not to be endured; he admitted the metre was perfect, and there wasn't a single false rhyme. But the prose novelette was disgusting. "It is such stuff," said he, "as little boys scribble upon walls."

I said I could not see anything objectionable in it.

"Come now, confess you are ashamed of it," he urged. "You only wrote it to make money."

"If you mean that I deliberately wrote low stuff to make money," I replied calmly, "it is untrue. There is nothing I am ashamed of. What you object to is simply realism." I pointed out that Bret Harte had been as realistic; but they did not understand literature on that committee.

"Confess you are ashamed of yourself," he reiterated, "and we will look over it."

"I am not," I persisted, though I foresaw only too clearly that my summer's vacation was doomed if I told the truth. "What is the use of saying I am?"

The headmaster uplifted his hands in horror. "How, after all your kindness to him, he can contradict you—!" he cried.

"When I come to be your age," I conceded to the member of the committee, "it is possible I may look back on it with shame. At present I feel none."

In the end I was given the alternative of expulsion or of publishing nothing which had not passed the censorship of the committee. After considerable hesitation I chose the latter.

This was a blessing in disguise; for, as I have never been able to endure the slightest arbitrary interference with my work, I simply abstained from publishing. Thus, although I still wrote—mainly sentimental verses—my nocturnal studies were less interrupted. Not till I had graduated, and was of age, did I return to my inky vomit. Then came my next first book—a real book at last.

In this also I had the collaboration of a fellow-teacher, Louis Cowen by name. This time my colleague was part-author. It was only gradually that I had been admitted to the privilege of communion with him, for he was my senior by five or six years, and a man of brilliant parts who had already won his spurs in journalism, and who enjoyed deservedly the reputation of an Admirable Crichton. What drew me to him was his mordant wit (today, alas! wasted on anonymous journalism! If he would only reconsider his indetermination, the reading public would be the richer!) Together we planned plays, novels, treatises on political economy, and contributions to philosophy. Those were the days of dreams.

One afternoon he came to me with quivering sides, and told me that an idea for a little shilling book had occurred to him. It was that a Radical Prime Minister and a Conservative working man should change into each other by supernatural means, and the working man be confronted with the problem of governing, while the Prime Minister should be as comically out of place in the East End environment. He thought it would make a funny "Arabian Nights" sort of burlesque. And so it would have done; but, unfortunately, I saw subtler possibilities of political satire in it, nothing less than a *reductio ad absurdum* of the whole system of Party Government. I insisted the story must be real, not supernatural, the Prime Minister must be a Tory, weary of office, and it must be an ultra-Radical atheistic artisan bearing a marvellous resemblance to him who directs (and with complete success) the Conservative Administration. To add to the mischief, owing to my collaborator's evenings being largely taken up by other work, seven-eighths of the book came to be written by me, though the leading ideas were, of course, threshed out and the whole revised in common, and thus it became a vent-hole for all the ferment of a youth of twenty-one, whose literary faculty had furthermore been pent up for years by the potential censorship of a committee. The book, instead of being a shilling skit, grew to a ten-and-sixpenny (for that was the unfortunate price of publication) political treatise of over sixty long chapters and 500 closely printed pages. I drew all the characters as seriously and complexly as if the fundamental conception were a matter of history; the outgoing Premier became an elaborate study of a nineteenth-century Hamlet; the Bethnal Green life amid which he came to live was presented with photographic fulness and my old trick of realism; the governmental manoeuvres were described with infinite detail; numerous real personages were introduced under nominal disguises; and subsequent history was curiously anticipated in some of the Female Franchise and Home Rule episodes. Worst of all, so super-subtle was the satire, that it was never actually stated straight out that the Premier had changed places with the Radical working man, so that the door might be left open for satirically suggested alternative explanations of the metamorphosis in their characters; and as, moreover, the two men re-assumed their original *rôles* for one night only with infinitely complex effects, many readers, otherwise unimpeachable, reached the end without any suspicion of the actual plot—and yet (on their own confession) enjoyed the book!

In contrast to all this elephantine waggery the half-dozen chapters near the commencement, in which my collaborator sketched the first adventures of the Radical working man in Downing Street, were light and sparkling, and I feel sure the shilling skit he originally meditated would have been a great success. We christened the book. "The Premier and the Painter," ourselves J. Freeman Bell, had it type-written, and sent it round to the publishers in two enormous quarto volumes. I had been working at it for more than a year every evening after the hellish torture of the day's teaching, and all day every holiday, but now I had a good rest while it was playing its boomerang prank of returning to me once a month. The only gleam of hope came from Bentleys, who wrote to say that they could not make up their minds to reject it; but they prevailed upon themselves to part with it at last, though not without asking to see Mr. Bell's next book. At last it was accepted by Spencer Blackett, and, though it had been refused by all the best houses, it failed. Failed in a material sense, that is; for there was plenty of praise in the papers, though at too long intervals to do us any good. The *Athenæum* has never spoken so well of anything I have done since. The late James Runciman (I learnt after his death that it was he) raved about it in various uninfluential organs. It even called forth a leader in the *Family Herald*(!), and there are odd people here and there, who know the secret of J. Freeman Bell, who declare that I. Zangwill will never do anything so good. There was a cheaper edition, but it did not sell much then, though now it is in its third edition, issued uniformly with my other books by Heinemann, and absolutely unrevised. But not only did "The Premier and the Painter" fail with the great public at first, it did not even help either of us one step up the ladder; never got us a letter of encouragement nor a stroke of work. I had to begin journalism at the very bottom and entirely unassisted, narrowly escaping canvassing for advertisements, for I had by this time thrown up my scholastic position, and had gone forth into the world penniless and without even a "character," branded as an Atheist (because I did not worship the Lord who presided over our committee) and a Revolutionary (because I refused to break the law of the land).

I should stop here if I were certain I had written the required article. But as "The Premier and the Painter" was not entirely *my* first book, I may perhaps be expected to say something of my third first book, and the first to which I put my name—"The Bachelors' Club." Years of literary apathy succeeded the failure of "The Premier and the Painter." All I did was to publish a few serious poems (which, I hope, will survive *Time*), a couple of pseudonymous stories signed "The Baroness Von S."(!), and a long philosophical essay upon religion, and to lend a hand in the writing of a few playlets. Becoming convinced of the irresponsible mendacity of the dramatic profession, I gave up the stage, too, vowing never to write except on commission (I kept my vow and yet was played ultimately), and sank entirely into the slough of journalism (glad enough to get there), *inter alia* editing a comic paper (not *Grimaldi*, but *Ariel*) with a heavy heart. At last the long apathy wore off, and I resolved to cultivate literature again in my scraps of time. It is a mere accident that I wrote a pair of "funny" books, or put serious criticism of contemporary manners into a shape not understood in a country where only the dull are profound and only the ponderous are earnest. "The Bachelors' Club" was the result of a whimsical remark made by my dear friend, Eder of Bartholomew's, with whom I was then sharing rooms in Bernard Street, and who helped me greatly with it, and its publication was equally accidental. One spring day, in the year of grace 1891, having lived unsuccessfully for a score of years and seven upon this absurd planet, I crossed Fleet Street and stepped into what is called "success." It was like this. Mr. J. T. Grein, now of the Independent Theatre, meditated a little monthly called *The Playgoers' Review*, and he asked me to do an article for the first number, on the strength of some speeches I had made at the Playgoers' Club.

When I got the proof it was marked, "Please return at once to 6 Bouverie Street." My office boy being out, and Bouverie Street being only a few steps away, I took it over myself, and found myself, somewhat to my surprise, in the office of Henry & Co., publishers, and in the presence of Mr. J. Hannaford Bennett, an active partner in the firm. He greeted me by name, also to my surprise, and told me he had heard me speak at the Playgoers' Club. A little conversation ensued, and he mentioned that his firm was going to bring out a Library of Wit and Humour. I told him I had begun a book, avowedly humorous, and had written two chapters of it, and he straightway came over to my office, heard me read them, and immediately secured the book. (The then editor ultimately refused to have it in the "Whitefriars' Library of Wit and Humour," and so it was brought out separately.) Within three months, working in odds and ends of time, I finished it, correcting the proofs of the first chapters while I was writing the last; indeed, ever since the day I read those two chapters to Mr. Hannaford Bennett I have never written a line anywhere that has not been purchased before it was written. For, to my undying astonishment, two average editions of my real "first book" were disposed of on the day of publication, to say nothing of the sale in New York. Unless I had acquired a reputation of which I was totally unconscious, it must have been the title that "fetched" the trade. Or, perhaps, it was the illustrations by my friend, Mr. George Hutchinson, whom I am proud to have discovered as a cartoonist for *Ariel*.

So here the story comes to a nice sensational climax. Re-reading it, I feel dimly that there ought to be a moral in it somewhere for the benefit of struggling fellow-scribblers. But the best I can find is this: That if you are blessed with some talent, a great deal of industry, and an amount of conceit mighty enough to enable you to disregard superiors, equals and critics, as well as the fancied demands of the public, it is possible, without friends, or introductions, or bothering celebrities to read your manuscripts, or cultivating the camp of the log-rollers, to attain, by dint of slaving day and night for years during the flower of your youth, to a fame infinitely less widespread than a prizefighter's, and a pecuniary position which you might with far less trouble have been born to.

"The Western Avernus"

By Morley Roberts

C ertainly no one was more surprised than myself when I discovered that I could write decent prose, and even make money out of it, for during many years my youthful aspirations had been to rival Rossetti, or get on a level with Browning, rather than to make a living out of literature as a profession. But when I did start a book, I went through three years of American experience like fire through flax, and wrote "The Western Avernus," a volume containing ninety-three thousand words, in less than a lunar month.

I had been in Australia years before, coming home before the mast as an A.B. in a Blackwall liner, but my occasional efforts to turn that experience into form always failed. Once or twice, I read some of my prose to friends, who told me that it was worse even than my poetry. Such criticism naturally confirmed me in the belief that I must be a poet or nothing, and I soon got into a fair way to become nothing, for my health broke down. At last, finding my choice lay between two kinds of tragedies, I chose the least, and went off to Texas. On February 27, 1884, I was working in a Government office as a writer; on March 27, I was sheep-herding in Scurry County, North-west Texas, in the south of the Panhandle. This experience was the opening of "The Western Avernus."

But I should never have written the book if it had not been for two friends of mine. One was George Gissing, and the other W. H. Hudson, the Argentine naturalist. When I returned from the West, and yarned to them of starvation and toil and strife in that new world, they urged me to put it down instead of talking it. I suppose they looked on it as good material running to verbal conversational waste, being both writers of many years' standing. Now I understand their point of view, and carry a note-book, or an odd piece of paper, to jot down motives that crop up in occasional talk, but then I was ignorant, and astonished at the wild notion of writing anything saleable. However, in desperation, for I had no money, I began to write, and went ahead in the same way that I have so far kept to. I wrote it without notes, without care, without thought, save that each night the past was resurgent and alive before and within me, just as it was when I worked and starved between Texas and the great North-west. Each Sunday I read what I had done to George Gissing; at first with terror, but afterwards with more confidence when he nodded approval, and as the end approached I began to believe in it myself.

It is only six years since the book was finished and sent to Messrs. Smith, Elder, & Co., but it seems half a century ago, so much has happened since then; and when it was accepted and published and paid for, and actually reviewed favourably, I almost determined to take to literature as a profession. I remembered that when I was a boy of eleven I wrote a romance with twenty people, men and women, in it. I married them all off at the end, being then in the childish mind of the most usual novelist who believes, or pretends to believe, or at any rate by implication teaches, that the interesting part of life finishes then instead of beginning. I recalled the fact that I wrote doggerel verse at the age of thirteen when I was at Bedford Grammar School, and that an ardent, ignorant Conservatism drove me, when I was at Owens College, Manchester, to lampoon the Liberal candidates in rhymes, and paste them up in the big lavatory; and under the influence of these memories I began to think that perhaps scribbling was my natural trade. I had tried some forty different callings, including "sailorising," saw-mill work, bullock-driving, tramping, and the selling of books in San Francisco, with indifferent financial success, so perhaps my *métier* was the making of books instead. So I went on trying, and had a very bad time for two years.

Having written "The Western Avernus" in a kind of intuitive, instructive way, it came easy enough to me, but very soon I began to think of the technique of writing, and wrote badly. I had to look back at the best part of that book to be assured I could write at all. For a long time it was a consolation and a distress to me, for I had to find out that knowledge must get into one's fingers before it can be used. Only those who know nothing, or who know a great deal very well, can write decently, and the intermediate state is exceedingly painful. Both the public and private laudation of my American book made me unhappy then. I thought I had only that one book in me.

Some of the letters I received from America, and, more particularly, British Columbia, were anything but cheerful reading. One man, of whom I had spoken rather freely, said I should be hanged on a cottonwood tree if I ever set foot in the Colony again. I do not believe there are any cottonwoods there, but he used a phrase common in

American literature. Another whilom friend of mine, who had read some favourable criticisms, wrote me to say he was sure Messrs. Smith & Elder had paid for them. He had understood it was always done, and now he knew the truth of it, because the book was so bad. I almost feared to return to British Columbia: the critics there might use worse weapons than a sneering paragraph. In England the worst one need fear is an action for criminal libel, or a rough and tumble fight. There it might end in an inquest. I wrote back to my critics that if I ever came out again, I would come armed, and endeavour to reply effectually.

For that wild life, far away from the ancient set and hardened bonds of social law which crush a man and make him just like his fellows, or so nearly like that only intimacy can distinguish individual differences, had allowed me to grow in another way, and become more myself; more independent, more like a savage, better able to fight and endure. That is the use of going abroad, and going abroad to places that are not civilised. They allow a man to revert and be himself. It may make his return hard, his endurance of social bonds bitterer, but it may help him to refuse to endure. He may attain to some natural sight.

Not many weeks ago I was talking to a well-known American publisher, and our conversation ran on the trans-oceanic view of Europe. He was amused and delighted to come across an Englishman who was so Americanised in one way as to look on our standing camps and armed kingdoms as citizens of the States do, especially those who live in the West. To the American, Europe seems like a small collection of walled yards, each with a crowing fighting-cock defying the universe on the top of his own dunghill, with an occasional scream from the wall. The whole of our international politics gets to look small and petty, and a bitter waste of power. Perhaps the American view is right. At any rate, it seemed so when I sat far aloof upon the lofty mountains to the west of the great plains. The isolation from the politics of the moment allowed me to see nature and natural law.

And as it was with nations, so it was with men. Out yonder, in the West, most of us were brutal at times, and ready to kill, or be killed, but my American-bred acquaintances looked like men, strikingly like men, independent, free, equal to the need of the ensuing day or the call of some sudden hour. It is a liberal education to the law-abiding Englishman to see a good specimen of a Texan cowboy walk down a Western street; for he looks like a law unto himself, calm and greatly assured of the validity of his own enactments. We live in a crowd here, and it takes a rebel to be himself; and in the struggle for freedom he is likely to go under.

While I was gaining the experience that went solid and crystallised into "The Western Avernus," I was discovering much that had never been discovered before, not in a geographical sense—for I have been in few places where men have not been—but in myself. Each new task teaches us something new, and something more than the mere way to do it. To drive horses or milk a cow or make bread, or kill a sheep, sets us level with facts and face to face with some reality. We are called on to be real, and not the shadow of others. This is the worth that is in all real workers, whatever they do, under whatever conditions. Every truth so learnt strips away ancient falsehood from us; it is real education, not the taught instruction which makes us alike, and thus shams, merely arming us with weapons to fight our fellows in the crowded, unwholesome life of falsely civilised cities.

And in America there is the sharp contrast between the city life and the life of the mountain and the plain. It is seen more clearly than in England, which is all more or less city. There are no clear stellar interspaces in our life here. But out yonder, a long day's train ride across the high barren cactus plateaus of Arizona teaches us as much as a clear and open depth in the sky. For, of a sudden, we run into the very midst of a big town, and shams are made gods for our worship. It is difficult to be oneself when all others refuse to be themselves.

This was for me the lesson of the West and the life there. When I wrote this book I did not know it; I wrote almost unconsciously, without taking thought, without weighing words, without conscious knowledge. But I see now what I learnt in a hard and bitter school.

For I acknowledge that the experience was at times bitterly painful. It is not pleasant to toil sixteen hours a day; it is not good to starve overmuch; it is not well to feel bitter for long months. And yet it is well and good and pleasant in the end to learn realities and live without lies. It is better to be a truthful animal than a civilised man, as things go. I learnt much from horses and cattle and sheep; the very prairie dogs taught me; the ospreys and the salmon they preyed on expressed truths. They didn't attempt to live on words, or the dust and ashes of dead things. They were themselves and no one else, and were not diseased with theories or a morbid altruism that is based on dependence.

This, I think, is the lesson I learnt from my own book. I did not know it when I wrote it. I never thought of writing it; I never meant to write anything; I only went to America because England and the life of London made me ill. If I could have lived my own life here I would have stayed, but the crushing combination of social forces drove me out. For fear of cutting my own throat I left, and took my chance with natural forces. To fight with nature makes men, to fight with society makes devils, or criminals, or martyrs, and sometimes a man may be all three. I preferred to revert to mere natural conditions for a time.

To lead such a life for a long time is to give up creeds, and to go to the universal storehouse whence all creeds come. It is giving up dogmas and becoming religious. In true opposition to instructive nature, we find our own natural religion, which cannot be wholly like any other. So a life of this kind does not make men good, in the common sense of the word. But it makes a man good for something. It may make him an ethical outcast, as facts faced always will. He prefers induction to deduction, especially the sanctioned unverified deductions of social order. For nature affords the only verification for the logical process of deduction. "We fear nature too much, to say the least." For most of us hold to other men's theories instead of making our own.

When Mill said, "Solitude, in the sense of being frequently alone, is necessary to the formation of any depth of character," he spoke almost absolute truth. But here we can never be alone; the very air is full of the dead breath of others. I learnt more in a four days' walk over the California coast range, living on parched Indian corn, than I could have done in a lifetime of the solitude of a lonely house. The Selkirks and the Rocky Mountains are books of ancient learning: the long plains of grey grass, the burnt plateaus of the hot South, speak eternal truths to all who listen. They need not listen, for there men do not learn by the ear. They breathe the knowledge in.

In speaking as I have done about America I do not mean to praise it as a State or a society. In that respect it is perhaps worse than our own, more diseased, more under the heel of the money fiend, more recklessly and brutally acquisitive. But there are parts of it still more or less free; nature reigns still over vast tracts in the West. As a democracy it is so far a failure, as democracies must be organised on a plutocratic basis; but it at any rate allows a man to think himself a man. Walt Whitman is the big expression of that thought, but his fervent belief in America was really but deep trust in man himself, in man's power of revolt, in his ultimate recognition of the beauty of the truth. The power of America to teach lies in the fact that a great part of her fertile and barren soil has not yet been taught, not yet cultivated for the bread which of itself can feed no man wholly.

Perhaps among the few who have read "The Western Avernus" (for it was not a financial success), fewer still have seen what I think I myself see in it now. But it has taken me six years to understand it, six years to know how I came to write it, and what it meant. That is the way in life: we do not learn at once what we are taught, we do not always understand all we say even when speaking earnestly. There is often one aspect of a book that the writer himself can learn from, and that is not always the technical part of it. All sayings may have an esoteric meaning. In those hard days by the camp fire, on the trail, on the prairie with sheep and cattle, I did not understand that they called up in me the ancient underlying experience of the race, and, like a deep plough, brought to the surface the lowest soil which should hereafter be a little fertile. When I starved, I thought not of our far ancestors who had suffered too; as I watched the sheep or the sharp-horned Texas steers, I could not reflect upon our pastoral forefathers; as I climbed with bleeding feet the steep slopes of the Western hills, my thoughts were set in a narrow circle of dark misery. I could not think of those who had striven, like me, in distant ages. But the songs of the camp fire, and the leap of the flame, and the crackling wood, and the lofty snow-clad hills, and the long dim plains, the wild beast, and the venomous serpents, and the need of food, brought me back to nature, the nature that had created those who were the fathers of us all, and, bringing me back, they taught me, as they strive to teach all, that the real and deeper life is everywhere, even in a city, if we will but look for it with unsealed eyes and minds set free from the tedious trivialities of this debauched modern life.

"A Life's Atonement"

By David Christie Murray

I began my first book more years ago than I care to count, and, naturally enough, it took poetic form, if not poetic substance. In its original shape it was called "Marsh Hall," and ran into four cantos. On the eve of my twenty-first birthday I sent the MS. to Messrs. Macmillan, who, very wisely, as I have since come to believe, counselled me not to publish it. I say this in full sincerity, though I remember some of the youthful bombast not altogether without affection. Here and there I can recall a passage which still seems respectable. I wrote reams of verse in those days, but when I came into the rough and tumble of journalistic life I was too occupied to court the Muses any longer, and found myself condemned to a life of prose. I was acting as special correspondent for the *Birmingham Morning News* in the year '73—I think it was '73, though it might have been a year later—and at that time Mr. Edmund Yates was lecturing in America, and a novel of his, the last he ever wrote, was running through our columns. Whether the genial "Atlas," who at that time had not taken the burden of *The World* upon his shoulders, found his associations too numerous and heavy, I can only guess, but he closed the story with an unexpected suddenness, and the editor, who had supposed himself to have a month or two in hand in which to make arrangements for his next serial, was confronted with the *finis* of Mr. Yates's work, and was compelled to start a new novel at a week's notice. In this extremity he turned to me. "I think, young 'un," he said, "that you ought to be able to write a novel." I shared his faith, and had, indeed, already begun a story which I had christened "Grace Forbeach." I handed him two chapters, which he read at once, and, in high feather, sent to the printer. It never bade fair to be a mighty work, but at least it fulfilled the meaning of the original edition of Pope's famous line, for it was certainly "all without a plan." I had appropriate scenery in my mind, no end of typical people to draw, and one or two moving actualities to work from. But I had forgotten the plot. To attempt a novel without a definite scheme of some sort is very like trying to make a Christmas pudding without a cloth. Ruth Pinch was uncertain as to whether her first venture at a pudding might not turn out a soup. My novelistic effort, I am sorry to confess, had no cohesion in it. Its parts got loose in the cooking, and I have reason to think that most people who tried it found the dish repellent. The cashier assured me that I had sent down the circulation of the Saturday issue by sixteen thousand. I had excellent reasons for disbelieving this circumstantial statement in the fact that the Saturday issue had never reached that number, but I have no doubt I did a deal of damage. There had been an idea in "Marsh Hall," and what with interpolated ballads and poetic excursions and alarums of all sorts, I had found in it matter enough to fill out my four cantos. I set out with the intent to work that same idea through the pages of "Grace Forbeach," but it was too scanty for the uses of a three-volume novel, at least in the hands of a tiro. I know one or two accomplished gentlemen who could make it serve the purpose admirably, and, perhaps, I myself might do something with it at a pinch at this time of day. Anyhow, as it was, the cloth was too small to hold the pudding, and, in the process of cooking, I was driven to the most desperate expedients. To drop the simile and to come to the plain facts of the case, I sent all my wicked and superfluous people into a coal-mine, and there put an end to them by an inrush of water. I forget what became of the hero, but I know that some of the most promising characters dropped out of that story, and were no more heard of. The sub-editor used occasionally, for my encouragement, to show me letters he received, denouncing the work, and asking wrathfully when it would end.

Whilst I am about "Grace Forbeach," it may be worth while to tell the story of the champion printer's error of my experience. I wrote at the close of the story:

> *"Are there no troubles now?" the lover asks.*
> *"Not one, dear Frank. Not one."*
> *And then, in brackets, thus () I set the words:*
> *(White line.)*

This was a technical instruction to the printer, and meant that one line of space should be left clear. The genius who had the copy in hand put the lover's speech in type correctly, and then, setting it out as if it were a line of verse, he gave me—

> *"Not one, dear Frank, not one white line!"*

It was a custom in the printing office to suspend a leather medal by a leather bootlace round the neck of the man who had achieved the prize *bêtise* of the year. It was somewhere about midsummer at this time, but it was instantly and unanimously resolved that nothing better than this would or could be done by anybody. The compositors performed what they called a "jerry" in the blunderer's honour, and invested him, after an animated fight, with the medal.

"Grace Forbeach" has been dead and buried for very nearly a score of years. It never saw book form, and I was never anxious that it should do so, but as *it* had grown out of "Marsh Hall," so my first book grew out of it, and, oddly enough, not only my first, but my second and my third. "Joseph's Coat," which made my fortune, and gave me such literary standing as I have, was built on one episode of that abortive story, and "Val Strange" was constructed and written to lead up to the episode of the attempted suicide on Welbeck Head, which had formed the culminating point in the poem.

When I got to London I determined to try my hand anew, and, having learned by failure something more than success could ever have taught me, I built up my scheme before I started on my book. Having come to utter grief for want of a scheme to work on, I ran, in my eagerness to avoid that fault, into the opposite extreme, and built an iron-bound plot, which afterwards cost me very many weeks of unnecessary and unvalued labour. I am quite sure that no reader of "A Life's Atonement" ever guessed that the author took one tithe, or even one-twentieth part, of the trouble it actually cost to weave the two strands of its narrative together. I divided my story into thirty-six chapters. Twelve of these were autobiographical, in the sense that they were supposed to be written by the hero in person. The remaining twenty-four were historical, purporting to be written, that is, by an impersonal author. The autobiographical portions necessarily began in the childhood of the narrator, and between them and the "History" there was a considerable gulf of time. Little by little this gulf had to be bridged over until the action in both portions of the story became synchronous. I really do not suppose that the most pitiless critic ever felt it worth his while to question the accuracy of my dates, and I dare say that all the trouble I took was quite useless, but I fixed in my own mind the actual years over which the story extended, and spent scores of hours in the consultation of old almanacs. I have never verified the work since it was done, but I believe that in this one respect, at least, it is beyond cavil. The two central figures of the book were lifted straight from the story of "Marsh Hall," and "Grace Forbeach" gave her quota to the narrative.

I had completed the first volume when I received a commission to go out as special correspondent to the Russo-Turkish war. I left the MS. behind me, and for many months the scheme was banished from my mind. I went through those cities of the dead, Kesanlik, Calofar, Carlova, and Sopot. I watched the long-drawn artillery duel at the Shipka Pass, made the dreary month-long march in the rainy season from Orkhanié to Plevna, with the army of reinforcement, under Chefket Pasha and Chakir Pasha, lived in the besieged town until Osman drove away all foreign visitors, and sent out his wounded to sow the whole melancholy road with corpses. I put up on the heights of Tashkesen, and saw the stubborn defence of Mehemet Ali, and there was pounced upon by the Turkish authorities for a too faithful dealing with the story of the horrors of the war, and was deported to Constantinople. I had originally gone out for an American journal at the instance of a gentleman who exceeded his instructions in despatching me, and I was left high and dry in the Turkish capital without a penny and without a friend. But work of the kind I could do was wanted, and I was on the spot. I slid into an engagement with the *Scotsman*, and then into another with the *Times*. The late Mr. Macdonald, who was killed by the Pigott forgeries, was then manager of the leading journal, and offered me fresh work. I waited for it, and a year of wild adventure in the face of war had given me such a taste for that sort of existence that I let "A Life's Atonement" slide, and had no thought of taking it up again. A misunderstanding with the *Times* authorities—happily cleared up years after—left me in the cold, and I was bound to do something for a living. The first volume of "A Life's Atonement" had been written in the intervals of labour in the Gallery of the House of Commons, and such work as an active hack journalist can find among the magazines and the weekly society papers. I had been away a whole year, and everywhere my place was filled. It was obviously no use to a man in want of ready money to undertake the completion of a three-volume novel of which only one volume was written, and so I betook myself to the writing of short stories. The very first of these was blessed by a lucky accident. Mr. George Augustus Sala had begun to write for *The Gentleman's Magazine* a story called, if I remember rightly, "Dr. Cupid." Sala was suddenly summoned by the proprietors of the *Daily Telegraph* to undertake one of his innumerable journeys, and the copy of the second instalment of his story reached the editor too late for publication. Just when the publishers of the *Gentleman's* were at a loss for suitable copy, my MS. of "An Old Meerschaum" reached them, and, to my delighted surprise, I received proofs almost by return of post. The story appeared, with an illustration by Arthur Hopkins, and, about a week later, there came to me, through Messrs. Chatto & Windus, a letter from Robert Chambers: "Sir,—I have read, with unusual pleasure and interest, in this month's *Gentleman's Magazine*, a story from your pen entitled 'An Old Meerschaum.' If you have a novel on hand, or in preparation, I should be glad to see it. In the meantime, a short story, not much longer than 'An Old Meerschaum,' would be gladly considered by—Yours very truly, ROBERT CHAMBERS. P.S.—We publish no authors' names, but we pay handsomely." This letter brought back to mind at once the neglected "Life's Atonement," but I was uncertain as to the whereabouts of the MS. I searched everywhere amongst my own belongings in vain, but it suddenly occurred to me that I had left it in charge of a passing acquaintance of mine, who had taken up the unexpired lease of my chambers in Gray's Inn at the time of my departure for the seat of war. I jumped into a cab, and drove off in search of my property. The shabby old laundress who had made my bed and served my breakfast was pottering about the rooms. She remembered me perfectly well, of course, but could not remember that I had left anything behind me when I went away. I talked of manuscript, and she recalled doubtfully a quantity of waste paper, of the final destination of which she knew nothing. I began to think it extremely improbable that I should ever recover a line of the missing novel, when she opened a cupboard and drew from it a brown-paper parcel, and, opening it, displayed to me the MS. of which I was in search. I took it home and read it through with infinite misgiving. The enthusiasm with which I had begun the work had long since had time to pall, and the whole thing looked weary, flat, stale, and unprofitable. For one thing, I had adopted the abominable expedient of writing in the present tense so far as the autobiographical portion of the work was concerned, and, in the interval which had gone by, my taste had, I suppose, undergone an unconscious correction. It was a dull business, but, despondent as I was, I found the heart to rewrite those chapters. Charles Reade describes the task of writing out one's work a second time as "nauseous," and I confess that I am with him with all my heart. It is a misery which I have never since, in all my work, imposed upon myself. At that time I counted amongst my friends an eminent novelist, on whose critical faculty and honesty I knew I could place the most absolute reliance. I submitted my revised first volume to his judgment, and was surprised to learn that he thought highly of it. His judgment gave me new courage, and I sent the copy in to Chambers. After a delay of a week or two, I received a letter which gave me, I think, a keener delight than has ever touched me at the receipt of any other communication. "If," wrote Robert Chambers, "the rest is as good as the first volume, I shall accept the book with pleasure. Our price for the serial use will be 250*l.*, of which we will pay 100*l.* on receipt of completed MS.; the remaining 150*l.* will be paid on the publication of the first monthly number." I had been out of harness for so long a time, and had been, by desultory work, able to earn so little, that this letter seemed to open a sort of Eldorado to my gaze. It was not that alone which made it so agreeable to receive. It opened the way to an honourable ambition which I had long nourished, and I slaved away at the remaining two volumes with an enthusiasm which I have never been able to revive. There are two or three people still extant who know in part the privations I endured whilst the book was being finished. I set everything else on one side for it, incautiously enough, and for two months I did not earn a penny by other means. The most trying accident of all the time was the tobacco famine which set in towards the close of the third volume, but, in spite of all obstacles, the book was finished. I worked all night at the final chapter, and wrote "Finis" somewhere about five o'clock on a summer morning. I shall never forget the solemn exultation with which I laid down my pen and looked from the window of the little room in which I had been working over the golden splendour of the gorse-covered common of Ditton Marsh. All my original enthusiasm had revived, and in the course of my lonely labours had grown to a white heat. I solemnly believed at that moment that I had written a great book. I suppose I may make that confession now without proclaiming myself a fool. I really and seriously believed that the work I had just finished was original in conception, style, and character. No reviewer ever taunted me with the fact, but the truth is that "A Life's Atonement" is a very curious instance of unconscious plagiarism. It is quite evident to my mind now that if there had been no "David Copperfield" there would have been no "Life's Atonement." My Gascoigne is Steerforth, my John Campbell is David, John's aunt is Miss Betsy Trotwood, Sally Troman is Peggotty. The very separation of the friends, though brought about by a different cause, is a reminiscence. I was utterly unconscious of these facts, and, remembering how devotedly and honestly I worked, how resolute I was to put my best of observation and invention into the story, I have ever since felt chary of entertaining a charge of plagiarism against anybody. There are, of course, flagrant and obvious cases, but I believe that in nine instances out of ten the supposed criminal has worked as I did, having so completely absorbed and digested in childhood the work of an admired master that he has come to feel that work as an actual portion of himself. "A Life's Atonement" ran its course through *Chambers's Journal* in due time, and was received with favour. Messrs. Griffith & Farran undertook its publication in book form, but one or two accidental circumstances forbade it to prosper in their hands. To begin with, the firm at that time had only newly decided on publishing novels at all, and a work under such a title, and issued by such a house, was naturally supposed to have a theological tendency. Then again, in the very week in which my book saw the light, "Lothair" appeared, and for the time being swamped everything. All the world read "Lothair," all the world talked about it, and all the newspapers and reviews dealt with it, to the exclusion of the products of the smaller fry. Later on, "A Life's Atonement" was handsomely reviewed, and was indeed, as I am disposed to think, praised a good deal beyond its merits. But it lay a dead weight on the hands of its original publishers, until Messrs. Chatto & Windus expressed a wish to incorporate it in their Piccadilly Series. The negotiations between the two houses were easily completed, the stock was transferred from one establishment to the other, the volumes were stripped of their old binding and dressed anew, and with this novel impetus the story reached a second edition in three-volume form. It brought me almost immediately two commissions, and by the time that they were completed I had grown into a professional novel-writer.

"A Romance of Two Worlds"

By Marie Corelli

It is an unromantic thing for an author to have had no literary vicissitudes. One cannot expect to be considered interesting, unless one has come up to London with the proverbial solitary "shilling," and gone about hungry and footsore, begging from one hard-hearted publisher's house to another with one's perpetually rejected manuscript under one's arm. One ought to have consumed the "midnight oil"; to have "coined one's heart's blood" (to borrow the tragic expression of a contemporary gentleman-novelist); to have sacrificed one's self-respect by metaphorically crawling on all-fours to the critical faculty; and to have become æsthetically cadaverous and blear-eyed through the action of inspired dyspepsia. Now, I am obliged to confess that I have done none of these things, which, to quote the Prayer-book, I ought to have done. I have had no difficulty in making my career or winning my public. And I attribute my good fortune to the simple fact that I have always tried to write straight from my own heart to the hearts of others, regardless of opinions and indifferent to results. My object in writing has never been, and never will be, to concoct a mere story which shall bring me in a certain amount of cash or notoriety, but solely because I wish to say something which, be it ill or well said, is the candid and independent expression of a thought which I will have uttered at all risks.

In this spirit I wrote my first book, "A Romance of Two Worlds," now in its seventh edition. It was the simply worded narration of a singular psychical experience, and included certain theories on religion which I, personally speaking, accept and believe. I had no sort of literary pride in my work whatsoever; there was nothing of self in the wish I had, that my ideas, such as they were, should reach the public, for I had no particular need of money, and certainly no hankering after fame. When the book was written I doubted whether it would ever find a publisher, though I determined to try and launch it if possible. My notion was to offer it to Arrowsmith as a shilling railway volume, under the title "Lifted Up." But in the interim, as a kind of test of its merit or demerit, I sent the MS. to Mr. George Bentley, head of the long-established and famous Bentley publishing firm. It ran the gauntlet of his "readers" first, and they all advised its summary rejection. Among these "readers" at that time was Mr. Hall Caine. His strictures on my work were peculiarly bitter, though, strange to relate, he afterwards forgot the nature of his own report. For, on being introduced to me at a ball given by Miss Eastlake, when my name was made and my success assured, he blandly remarked, before a select circle of interested auditors, that he "had had the pleasure of *recommending*" my first book to Mr. Bentley! Comment on this were needless and unkind: he tells stories so admirably that I readily excuse him for his "slip of memory," and accept the whole incident as a delightful example of his inventive faculty.

His severe judgment pronounced upon me, combined with similar, but perhaps milder, severity on the part of the other "readers," had, however, an unexpected result. Mr. George Bentley, moved by curiosity, and possibly by compassion for the impending fate of a young woman so "sat upon" by his selected censors, decided to read my MS. himself. Happily for me, the consequence of his unprejudiced and impartial perusal was acceptance; and I still keep the kind and encouraging letter he wrote to me at the time, informing me of his decision, and stating the terms of his offer. These terms were, a sum down for one year's rights, the copyright of the work to remain my own entire property. I did not then understand what an advantage this retaining of my copyright in my own possession was to prove to me, financially speaking; but I am willing to do Mr. Bentley the full justice of supposing that he foresaw the success of the book; and that, therefore, his action in leaving me the sole owner of my then very small literary estate redounds very much to his credit, and is an evident proof amongst many of his manifest honour and integrity. Of course, the copyright of an unsuccessful book is valueless; but my "Romance" was destined to prove a sound investment, though I never dreamed that it would be so. Glad of my chance of reaching the public with what I had to say, I gratefully closed with Mr. Bentley's proposal. He considered the title "Lifted Up" as lacking attractiveness; it was therefore discarded, and Mr. Eric Mackay, the poet, gave the book its present name, "A Romance of Two Worlds."

Once published, the career of the "Romance" became singular, and totally apart from that of any other so-called "novel." It only received four reviews, all brief and distinctly unfavourable. The one which appeared in the dignified *Morning Post* is a fair sample of the rest. I keep it by me preciously, because it serves as a wholesome tonic to my mind, and proves to me that when a leading journal can so "review" a book, one need fear nothing from the literary knowledge, acumen, or discernment of reviewers. I quote it *verbatim*: "Miss Corelli would have been better advised had she embodied her ridiculous ideas in a sixpenny pamphlet. The names of Heliobas and Zara are alone sufficient indications of the dulness of this book." This was all. No explanation was vouchsafed as to why my ideas were "ridiculous," though such explanation was justly due; nor did the reviewer state why he (or she) found the "names" of characters "sufficient indications" of dulness, a curious discovery which I believe is unique. However, the so-called "critique" did one good thing; it moved me to sincere laughter, and showed me what I might expect from the critical brethren in these days—days which can no longer boast of a Lord Macaulay, a brilliant, if bitter, Jeffrey, or a generous Sir Walter Scott.

To resume: the four "notices" having been grudgingly bestowed, the Press "dropped" the "Romance," considering, no doubt, that it was "quashed," and would die the usual death of "women's novels," as they are contemptuously called, in the prescribed year. But it did nothing of the sort. Ignored by the Press, it attracted the public. Letters concerning it and its theories began to pour in from strangers in all parts of the United Kingdom; and at the end of its twelvemonth's run in the circulating libraries Mr. Bentley brought it out in one volume in his "Favorite" series. Then it started off at full gallop—the "great majority" got at it, and, what is more, kept at it. It was "pirated" in America; chosen out and liberally paid for by Baron Tauchnitz for the "Tauchnitz" series; translated into various languages on the Continent, and became a topic of social discussion. A perfect ocean of correspondence flowed in upon me from India, Africa, Australia, and America, and at this very time I count through correspondence a host of friends in all parts of the world whom I do not suppose I shall ever see; friends who even carry their enthusiasm so far as to place their houses at my disposal for a year or two years—and surely the force of hospitality can no further go! With all these attentions, I began to find out the advantage my practical publisher had given me in the retaining of my copyright; my "royalties" commenced, increased, and accumulated with every quarter, and at the present moment continue still to accumulate, so much so, that the "Romance of Two Worlds" alone, apart from all my other works, is the source of a very pleasant income. And I have great satisfaction in knowing that its prolonged success is not due to any influence save that which is contained within itself. It certainly has not been helped on by the Press, for since I began my career six years ago, I have never had a word of open encouragement or kindness from any leading English critic. The only real "reviews" I ever received worthy of the name appeared in the *Spectator* and the *Literary World*. The first was on my book "Ardath: The Story of a Dead Self," and in this the over-abundant praise in the beginning was all smothered by the unmitigated abuse at the end. The second in the *Literary World* was eminently generous; it dealt with my last book, "The Soul of Lilith." So taken aback was I with surprise at receiving an all-through kindly, as well as scholarly, criticism from any quarter of the Press, that, though I knew nothing about the *Literary World*, I wrote a letter of thanks to my unknown reviewer, begging the editor to forward it in the right direction. He did so, and my generous critic turned out to be—a woman—a literary woman, too, fighting a hard fight herself, who would have had an excuse to "slate" me as an unrequired rival in literature had she so chosen, but who, instead of this easy course, adopted the more difficult path of justice and unselfishness.

After the "Romance of Two Worlds" I wrote "Vendetta"; then followed "Thelma," and then "Ardath: The Story of a Dead Self," which, among other purely personal rewards, brought me a charming autograph letter from the late Lord Tennyson, full of valuable encouragement. Then followed "Wormwood: A Drama of Paris"—now in its fifth edition; "Ardath" and "Thelma" being in their seventh editions. My publishers seldom advertise the number of my editions, which is, I suppose, the reason why the continuous "run" of the books escapes the Press comment of the "great success" supposed to attend various other novels which only attain to third or fourth editions. "The Soul of Lilith," published only last year, ran through four editions in three-volume form; it is issued now in one volume by Messrs. Bentley, to whom, however, I have not offered any new work. A change of publishers is sometimes advisable; but I have a sincere personal liking for Mr. George Bentley, who is himself an author of distinct originality and ability, though his literary gifts are only known to his own private circle. His book of essays, entitled "After Business," is a delightful volume, full of point and brilliancy, two specially admirable papers being those on Villon and Carlyle, while it would be difficult to discover a more "taking" prose bit than the concluding chapter, "Under an Old Poplar."

A very foolish and erroneous rumour has of late been circulated concerning me, asserting that I owe a great measure of my literary success to the kindly recognition and interest of the Queen. I take the present opportunity to clear up this perverse misunderstanding. My books have been running successfully through several editions for six years, and the much-commented-upon presentation of a complete set of them to Her Majesty took place only last year. If it were possible to regret the honour of the Queen's acceptance of these volumes, I should certainly have cause to do so, as the extraordinary spite and malice that has since been poured on my unoffending head has shown me a very bad side of human nature, which I am sorry to have seen. There is very little cause to envy me in this matter. I have but received the courteously formal thanks of the Queen and the Empress Frederick, conveyed through the medium of their ladies-in-waiting, for the special copies of the books their Majesties were pleased to admire; yet for this simple and quite ordinary honour I have been subjected to such forms of gratuitous abuse as I did not think possible to a "just and noble" English Press. I have often wondered why I was not equally assailed when the Queen of Italy, not content with merely "accepting" a copy of the "Romance of Two Worlds," sent me an autograph portrait of herself, accompanied by a charming letter, a souvenir which I value, not at all because the sender is a queen, but because she is a sweet and noble woman whose every action is marked by grace and unselfishness, and who has deservedly won the title given her by her people, "the blessing of Italy." I repeat, I owe nothing whatever of my popularity, such as it is, to any "royal" notice or favour, though I am naturally glad to have been kindly recognised and encouraged by those "throned powers" who command the nation's utmost love and loyalty. But my appeal for a hearing was first made to the great public, and the public responded; moreover, they do still respond with so much heartiness and goodwill, that I should be the most ungrateful scribbler that ever scribbled if I did not (despite Press "drubbings" and the amusing total ignoring of my very existence by certain cliquey literary magazines) take up my courage in both hands, as the French say, and march steadily onward to such generous cheering and encouragement.

I am told by an eminent literary authority that critics are "down upon me" because I write about the supernatural. I do not entirely believe the eminent literary authority, inasmuch as I have not always written about the supernatural. Neither "Vendetta," nor "Thelma," nor "Wormwood" is supernatural. But, says the eminent literary authority, why write at all, at anytime, about the supernatural? Why? Because I feel the existence of the supernatural, and feeling it, I must speak of it. I understand that the religion we profess to follow emanates from the supernatural. And I presume that churches exist for the solemn worship of the supernatural. Wherefore, if the supernatural be thus universally acknowledged as a guide for thought and morals, I fail to see why I, and as many others as choose to do so, should not write on the subject. An author has quite as much right to characterise angels and saints in his or her pages as a painter has to depict them on his canvas. And I do not keep my belief in the supernatural as a sort of special mood to be entered into on Sundays only; it accompanies me in my daily round, and helps me along in all my business. But I distinctly wish it to be understood that I am neither a "Spiritualist" nor a "Theosophist." I am not a "strong-minded" woman, with egotistical ideas of a "mission." I have no other supernatural belief than that which is taught by the Founder of our Faith, and this can never be shaken from me or "sneered down." If critics object to my dealing with this in my books, they are very welcome to do so; their objections will not turn me from what they are pleased to consider the error of my ways. I know that unrelieved naturalism and atheism are much more admired subjects with the critical faculty; but the public differ from this view. The public, being in the main healthy-minded and honest, do not care for positivism and pessimism. They like to believe in something better than themselves; they like to rest on the ennobling idea that there is a great loving Maker of this splendid Universe, and they have no lasting affection for any author whose tendency and teaching is to despise the hope of heaven, and "reason away" the existence of God. It is very clever, no doubt, and very brilliant to deny the Creator; it is as if a monkey should, while being caged and fed by man, deny man's existence. Such a circumstance would make us laugh, of course; we should think it uncommonly "smart" of the monkey. But we should not take his statement for a fact all the same.

Of the mechanical part of my work there is little to say. I write everyday from ten in the morning till two in the afternoon, alone and undisturbed, save for the tinpot tinkling of unmusical neighbours' pianos, and the perpetual organ-grinding which is freely permitted to interfere *ad libitum* with the quiet and comfort of all the patient brain-workers who pay rent and taxes in this great and glorious metropolis. I generally scribble off the first rough draft of a story very rapidly in pencil; then I copy it out in pen and ink, chapter by chapter, with fastidious care, not only because I like a neat manuscript, but because I think everything that is worth doing at all is worth doing well; and I do not see why my publishers should have to pay for more printers' errors than the printers themselves make necessary. I find, too, that in the gradual process of copying by hand, the original draft, like a painter's first sketch, gets improved and enlarged. No one sees my manuscript before it goes to press, as I am now able to refuse to submit my work to the judgment of "readers." These worthies treated me roughly in the beginning, but they will never have the chance again. I correct my proofs myself, though I regret to say my instructions and revisions are not always followed. In my novel "Wormwood" I corrected the French article "*le* chose" to "*la* chose" three times, but apparently the printers preferred their own French, for it is still "*le* chose" in the "Favorite" edition, and the error is stereotyped. In accordance with the arrangement made by Mr. George Bentley for my first book, I retain to myself sole possession of all my copyrights, and as all my novels are successes, the financial results are distinctly pleasing. America, of course, is always a thorn in the side of an author. The "Romance," "Vendetta," "Thelma" and "Ardath" were all "pirated" over there before the passing of the American Copyright Act, it being apparently out of Messrs. Bentley & Son's line to make even an attempt to protect my rights. After the Act was passed, I was paid a sum for "Wormwood," and a larger sum for "The Soul of Lilith," but, as everyone knows, the usual honorarium offered by American publishers for the rights of a successful English novel are totally inadequate to the sales they are able to command. American critics, however, have been very good to me. They have at least read my books before starting to review them, which is a great thing. I have always kept my "Tauchnitz" rights, and very pleasant have all my dealings been with the courteous and generous Baron. All wanderers on the Continent love the "Tauchnitz" volumes—their neatness, handy form, and remarkably clear type give them precedence over every other foreign series. Baron Tauchnitz pays his authors excellently well, and takes a literary as well as commercial interest in their fortunes.

Perhaps one of the pleasantest things connected with my "success" is the popularity I have won in many quarters of the Continent without any exertion on my own part. My name is as well known in Germany as anywhere, while in Sweden they have been good enough to elect me as one of their favourite authors, thanks to the admirable translations made of all my books by Miss Emilie Kullmann, of Stockholm, whose energy did not desert her even when she had so difficult a task to perform as the rendering of "Ardath" into Swedish. In Italy and Spain "Vendetta," translated into the languages of those countries, is popular. Madame Emma Guarducci-Giaconi is the translator of "Wormwood" into Italian, and her almost literal and perfect rendering has been running as the *feuilleton* in the Florentine journal, *La Nazione*, under the title "L'Alcoolismo: Un Dramma di Parigi." The "Romance of Two Worlds" is to be had in Russian, so I am told; and it will shortly be published at Athens, rendered into modern Greek. While engaged in writing this article, I have received a letter asking for permission to translate this same "Romance" into one of the dialects of North-west India, a request I shall very readily grant. In its Eastern dress the book will, I understand, be published at Lucknow. I may here state that I gain no financial advantage from these numerous translations, nor do I seek any. Sometimes the translators do not even ask my permission to translate, but content themselves with sending me a copy of the book when completed, without any word of explanation.

And now to wind up; if I have made a name, if I have made a career, as it seems I have, I have only one piece of pride connected with it. Not pride in my work, for no one with a grain of sense or modesty would, in these days, dare to consider his or her literary efforts of much worth, as compared with what has already been done by the past great authors. My pride is simply this: that I have fought my fight alone, and that I have no thanks to offer to anyone, save those legitimately due to the publisher who launched my first book, but who, it must be remembered, would, as a good business man, have unquestionably published nothing else of mine had I been a failure. I count no "friend on the Press," and I owe no "distinguished critic" any debt of gratitude. I have come, by happy chance, straight into close and sympathetic union with my public, and attained to independence and good fortune while still young and able to enjoy both. An "incomprehensibly successful" novelist I was called last summer by an irritated correspondent of *Life*, who chanced to see me sharing in the full flow of pleasure and social amusement during the "season" at Homburg. Well, if it be so, this "incomprehensible success" has been attained, I rejoice to say, without either "log-roller" or "boom," and were I of the old Greek faith, I should pour a libation to the gods for giving me this victory. Certainly I used to hope for what Britishers aptly call "fair play" from the critics, but I have ceased to expect that now. It is evidently a delight to them to abuse me, else they would not go out of their way to do it; and I have no wish to interfere with either their "copy" or their fun. The public are beyond them altogether. And Literature is like that famous hill told of in the "Arabian Nights," where threatening anonymous voices shouted the most deadly insults and injuries to anyone who attempted to climb it. If the adventurer turned back to listen, he was instantly changed into stone; but if he pressed boldly on, he reached the summit and found magic talismans. Now I am only at the commencement of the journey, and am ascending the hill with a light heart and in good humour. I hear the taunting voices on all sides, but I do not stop to listen, nor have I once turned back. My eyes are fixed on the distant peak of the mountain, and my mind is set on arriving there if possible. My ambition may be too great, and I may never arrive. That is a matter for the fates to settle. But, in the meanwhile, I enjoy climbing. I have nothing to grumble about. I consider Literature the noblest Art in the world, and have no complaint whatever to urge against it as a profession. Its rewards, whether great or small, are sufficient for me, inasmuch as I love my work, and love makes all things easy.

NOTE.—Since writing the above I have been asked to state whether, in my arrangements for publishing, I employ a "literary agent" or use a "type-writer." I do not. With regard to the first part of the query, I consider that authors, like other people, should learn how to manage their own affairs themselves, and that when they take a paid agent into their confidence, they make open confession of their business incapacity, and voluntarily elect to remain in foolish ignorance of the practical part of their profession. Secondly, I dislike type-writing, and prefer to make my own MS. distinctly legible. It takes no more time to write clearly than in spidery hieroglyphics, and a slovenly scribble is no proof of cleverness, but rather of carelessness and a tendency to "scamp" work.

"On the Stage and Off"

By Jerome K. Jerome

The story of one's "first book" I take to be the last chapter of one's literary romance. The long wooing is over. The ardent young author has at last won his coy public. The good publisher has joined their hands. The merry critics, invited to the feast of reason, have blessed the union, and thrown the rice and slippers—occasionally other things. The bridegroom sits alone with his bride, none between them, and ponders.

The fierce struggle, with its wild hopes and fears, its heart-leapings and heart-achings, its rose-pink dawns of endless promise, its grey twilights of despair, its passion and its pain, lies behind. Before him stretches the long, level road of daily doing. Will he please her to all time? Will she always be sweet and gracious to him? Will she never tire of him? The echo of the wedding-bells floats faintly through the darkening room. The fair forms of half-forgotten dreams rise up around him. He springs to his feet with a slight shiver, and rings for the lamps to be lighted.

Ah! that "first book" we meant to write! How it pressed forward an oriflamme of joy, through all ranks and peoples; how the world rang with the wonder of it! How men and women laughed and cried over it! From every page there leaped to light a new idea. Its every paragraph scintillated with fresh wit, deep thought, and new humour. And, ye gods! how the critics praised it! How they rejoiced over the discovery of the new genius! How ably they pointed out to the reading public its manifold merits, its marvellous charm! Aye, it was a great work, that book we wrote as we strode laughing through the silent streets, beneath the little stars.

And, heigho! what a poor little thing it was, the book that we did write! I draw him from his shelf (he is of a faint pink colour, as though blushing all over for his sins), and stand him up before me on the desk. "Jerome K. Jerome"—the K very big, followed by a small J, so that in many quarters the author is spoken of as "Jerome Kjerome," a name that in certain smoke-laden circles still clings to me—"On the Stage—and Off: The Brief Career of a would-be Actor. One Shilling."

I suppose I ought to be ashamed of him, but how can I be? Is he not my first-born? Did he not come to me in the days of weariness, making my heart glad and proud? Do I not love him the more for his shortcomings?

Somehow, as I stare at him in this dim candlelight, he seems to take odd shape. Slowly he grows into a little pink imp, sitting cross-legged among the litter of my books and papers, squinting at me (I think the squint is caused by the big "K"), and I find myself chatting with him.

It is an interesting conversation to me, for it is entirely about myself, and I do nearly all the talking, he merely throwing in an occasional necessary reply, or recalling to my memory a forgotten name or face.

We chat of the little room in Whitfield Street, off the Tottenham Court Road, where he was born; of our depressing, meek-eyed old landlady, and of how, one day, during the course of chance talk, it came out that she, in the far back days of her youth, had been an actress, winning stage love and breaking stage hearts with the best of them; of how the faded face would light up as, standing with the tea-tray in her hands, she would tell us of her triumphs, and repeat to us her "Press Notices," which she had learned by heart; and of how from her we heard not a few facts and stories useful to us. We talk of the footsteps that of evenings would climb the creaking stairs and enter at our door; of George, who always believed in us (God bless him!), though he could never explain why; of practical Charley, who thought we should do better if we left literature alone and stuck to work. Ah! well, he meant kindly, and there be many who would that he had prevailed. We remember the difficulties we had to contend with; the couple in the room below, who would come in and go to bed at twelve, and lie there, quarrelling loudly, until sleep overcame them about two, driving our tender and philosophical sentences entirely out of our head; of the asthmatical old law-writer, whose never-ceasing cough troubled us greatly (maybe, it troubled him also, but I fear we did not consider that); of the rickety table that wobbled as we wrote, and that, whenever in a forgetful moment we leant upon it, gently but firmly collapsed.

"Yes," I said to the little pink imp; 'as a study the room had its drawbacks, but we lived some grand hours there, didn't we? We laughed and sang there, and the songs we chose breathed ever of hope and victory, and so loudly we sang them we might have been modern Joshuas, thinking to capture a city with our breath.

"And then that wonderful view we used to see from its dingy window panes—that golden country that lay stretched before us, beyond the thousand chimney pots, above the drifting smoke, above the creeping fog—do you remember that?"

It was worth living in that cramped room, worth sleeping on that knobbly bed, to gain an occasional glimpse of that shining land, with its marble palaces, where one day we should enter, an honoured guest; its wide market-places, where the people thronged to listen to our words. I have climbed many stairs, peered through many windows in this London town since then, but never have I seen that view again. Yet, from somewhere in our midst, it must be visible for friends of mine, as we have sat alone, and the talk has sunk into low tones, broken by long silences, have told me that they, too, have looked upon those same glittering towers and streets. But the odd thing is that none of us has seen them since he was a very young man. So, maybe, it is only that the country is a long way off, and that our eyes have grown dimmer as we have grown older.

"And who was that old fellow that helped us so much?" I ask of my little pink friend; "you remember him surely—a very ancient fellow, the oldest actor on the boards he always boasted himself—had played with Edmund Kean and Macready. I used to put you in my pocket of a night and meet him outside the stage door of the Princess's; and we would adjourn to a little tavern in old Oxford Market to talk you over, and he would tell me anecdotes and stories to put in you."

"You mean Johnson," says the pink imp; "J. B. Johnson. He was with you in your first engagement at Astley's, under Murray Wood and Virginia Blackwood. He and you were the High Priests in 'Mazeppa,' if you remember, and had to carry Lisa Weber across the stage, you taking her head and he her heels. Do you recollect what he said to her, on the first night, as you were both staggering towards the couch?—'Well, I've played with Fanny Kemble, Cushman, Glyn, and all of them, but hang me, my dear, if you ain't the heaviest lead I've ever supported.'"

"That's the old fellow," I reply; "I owe a good deal to him, and so do you. I used to read bits of you to him in a whisper as we stood in the bar; and he always had one formula of praise for you: 'It's damned clever, young 'un; damned clever. I shouldn't have thought it of you.'"

"And that reminds me," I continue—I hesitate a little here, for I fear what I am about to say may offend him—"what have you done to yourself since I wrote you? I was looking you over the other day, and really I could scarcely recognise you. You were full of brilliancy and originality when you were in manuscript. What have you done with it all?"

By some mysterious process he contrives to introduce an extra twist into the squint with which he is regarding me, but makes no reply, and I continue:

"Take, for example, that gem I lighted upon one drizzly night in Portland Place. I remember the circumstance distinctly. I had been walking the deserted streets, working at you; my note-book in one hand and a pencil in the other. I was coming home through Portland Place, when suddenly, just beyond the third lamp-post from the Crescent, there flashed into my brain a thought so original, so deep, so true, that involuntarily I exclaimed: 'My God, what a grand idea!' and a coffee-stall keeper, passing with his barrow just at that moment, sang out: 'Tell it us, guv'nor. There ain't many knocking about.'

"I took no notice of the man, but hurried on to the next lamp-post to jot down that brilliant idea before I should forget it; and the moment I reached home I pulled you out of your drawer and copied it out on to your pages, and sat long staring at it, wondering what the world would say when it came to read it. Altogether I must have put into you nearly a dozen startlingly original thoughts. What have you done with them? They are certainly not there now."

Still he keeps silence, and I wax indignant at the evident amusement with which he regards my accusation.

"And the bright wit, the rollicking humour with which I made your pages sparkle, where are they?" I ask him, reproachfully; "those epigrammatic flashes that, when struck, illumined the little room with a blaze of sudden light, showing each cobweb in its dusty corner, and dying out, leaving my dazzled eyes groping for the lamp; those grand jokes at which I myself, as I made them, laughed till the rickety iron bedstead beneath me shook in sympathy with harsh metallic laughter; where are they, my friend? I have read you through, page by page, and the thoughts in you are thoughts that the world has grown tired of thinking; at your wit one smiles, thinking that anyone could think it wit; and your humour your severest critic could hardly accuse of being very new. What has happened to you? What wicked fairy has bewitched you? I poured gold into your lap, and you yield me back only crumpled leaves."

With a jerk of his quaint legs he assumes a more upright posture.

"My dear Parent," he begins in a tone that at once reverses our positions, so that he becomes the monitor and I the wriggling admonished; "don't, I pray you, turn prig in your old age; don't sink into the 'superior person' who mistakes carping for criticism, and jeering for judgment. Any fool can see faults, they lie on the surface. The merit of a thing is hidden within it, and is visible only to insight. And there is merit in me, in spite of your cheap sneers, sir. Maybe I do not contain an original idea. Show me the book published since the days of Caxton that does! Are our young men, as are the youth of China, to be forbidden to think, because Confucius thought years ago? The wit you appreciate now needs to be more pungent than the wit that satisfied you at twenty; are you sure it is as wholesome? You cannot smile at humour you would once have laughed at; is it you or the humour that has grown old and stale? I am the work of a very young man, who, writing of that which he knew and had felt, put down all things truthfully as they appeared to him, in such way as seemed most natural to him, having no thought of popular taste, standing in no fear of what critics might say. Be sure that all your future books are as free from unworthy aims."

"Besides," he adds, after a short pause, during which I have started to reply, but have turned back to think again, "is not this talk idle between you and me? This apologetic attitude, is it not the cant of the literary profession? At the bottom of your heart you are proud of me, as every author is of every book he has written. Some of them he thinks better than others; but, as the Irishman said of whiskies, they are all good. He sees their shortcomings. He dreams he could have done better; but he is positive no one else could."

His little twinkling eyes look sternly at me, and, feeling that the discussion is drifting into awkward channels, I hasten to divert it, and we return to the chat about our early experiences.

I ask him if he remembers those dreary days when, written neatly in round hand on sermon paper, he journeyed a ceaseless round from newspaper to newspaper, from magazine to magazine, returning always soiled and limp to Whitfield Street, still further darkening the ill-lit room as he entered. Some would keep him for a month, making me indignant at the waste of precious time. Others would send him back by the next post, insulting me by their indecent haste. Many, in returning him, would thank me for having given them the privilege and pleasure of reading him, and I would curse them for hypocrites. Others would reject him with no pretence at regret whatever, and I would marvel at their rudeness.

I hated the dismal little "slavey" who, twice a week, on an average, would bring him up to me. If she smiled as she handed me the packet,

I fancied she was jeering at me. If she looked sad, as she more often did, poor little over-worked slut, I thought she was pitying me. I shunned the postman if I saw him in the street, sure that he guessed my shame.

"Did anyone ever read you out of all those I sent you to?" I ask him.

"Do editors read manuscript by unknown authors?" he asks me in return.

"I fear not more than they can help," I confess; "they would have little else to do."

"Oh," he remarks demurely, "I thought I had read that they did."

"Very likely," I reply; "I have also read that theatrical managers read all the plays sent to them, eager to discover new talent. One obtains much curious information by reading."

"But somebody did read me eventually," he reminds me; "and liked me. Give credit where credit is due."

"Ah, yes," I admit; "my good friend Aylmer Gowing—the 'Walter Gordon' of the old Haymarket in Buckstone's time, 'Gentleman Gordon' as Charles Matthews nicknamed him—kindliest and most genial of men. Shall I ever forget the brief note that came to me four days after I had posted you to 'The Editor—*Play*':—'Dear Sir, I like your articles very much. Can you call on me tomorrow morning before twelve?— Yours truly, W. AYLMER GOWING.'"

So success had come at last—not the glorious goddess I had pictured, but a quiet, pleasant-faced lady. I had imagined the editor of *Cornhill*, or the *Nineteenth Century*, or *The Illustrated London News* writing me that my manuscript was the most brilliant, witty, and powerful story he had ever read, and enclosing me a cheque for two hundred guineas. *The Play* was an almost unknown little penny weekly, "run" by Mr. Gowing— who, though retired, could not bear to be altogether unconnected with his beloved stage—at a no inconsiderable yearly loss. It could give me little fame and less wealth. But a crust is a feast to a man who has grown weary of dreaming dinners, and as I sat with that letter in my hand a mist rose before my eyes, and I—acted in a way that would read foolish if written down.

The next morning, at eleven, I stood beneath the porch of 37 Victoria Road, Kensington, wishing I did not feel so hot and nervous, and that I had not pulled the bell-rope quite so vigorously. But when Mr. Gowing, in smoking-coat and slippers, came forward and shook me by the hand, my shyness left me. In his study, lined with theatrical books, we sat and talked. Mr. Gowing's voice seemed the sweetest I had ever listened to, for, with unprofessional frankness, it sang the praises of my work. He, in his young acting days, had been through the provincial mill, and found my pictures true, and many of my pages seemed to him, so he said, "as good as *Punch*." (He meant it complimentary.) He explained to me the position of his paper, and I agreed (only too gladly) to give him the use of the book for nothing. As I was leaving, however, he called me back and slipped a five-pound note into my hand—a different price from what friend A. P. Watt charms out of proprietors' pockets for me nowadays, yet never since have I felt as rich as on that foggy November morning when I walked across Kensington Gardens with that "bit of flimsy" held tight in my left hand. I could not bear the idea of spending it on mere mundane things. Now and then, during the long days of apprenticeship, I drew it from its hiding-place and looked at it, sorely tempted. But it always went back, and later, when the luck began to turn, I purchased with it, at a second-hand shop in Goodge Street, an old Dutch bureau that I had long had my eye upon. It is an inconvenient piece of furniture. One cannot stretch one's legs as one sits writing at it, and if one rises suddenly it knocks bad language into one's knees and out of one's mouth. But one must pay for sentiment, as for other things.

In *The Play* the papers gained a fair amount of notice, and won for me some kindly words; notably, I remember, from John Clayton and Palgrave Simpson. I thought that in the glory of print they would readily find a publisher, but I was mistaken. The same weary work lay before me, only now I had more heart in me, and, having wrestled once with Fate and prevailed, stood less in fear of her.

Sometimes with a letter of introduction, sometimes without, sometimes with a bold face, sometimes with a timid step, I visited nearly every publisher in London. A few received me kindly, others curtly, many not at all. From most of them I gathered that the making of books was a pernicious and unprofitable occupation. Some thought the work would prove highly successful if I paid the expense of publication, but were less impressed with its merits on my explaining to them my financial position. All kept me waiting long before seeing me, but made haste to say "Good day" to me.

I suppose all young authors have had to go through the same course. I sat one evening, a few months ago, with a literary friend of mine. The talk turned upon early struggles, and, with a laugh, he said: "Do you know one of the foolish things I love to do? I like to go with a paper parcel under my arm into some big publishing house, and to ask, in a low, nervous voice, if Mr. So-and-so is disengaged. The clerk, with a contemptuous glance towards me, says that he is not sure, and asks if I have an appointment. 'No,' I reply; 'not—not exactly, but I think he will see me. It's a matter of importance. I shall not detain him a minute.'"

"The clerk goes on with his writing, and I stand waiting. At the end of about five minutes, he, without looking up, says curtly, 'What name?' and I hand him my card.

"Up to that point, I have imagined myself a young man again, but there the fancy is dispelled. The man glances at the card, and then takes a sharp look at me. 'I beg your pardon, sir,' he says, 'will you take a seat in here for a moment?' In a few seconds he flies back again with 'Will you kindly step this way, sir?' As I follow him upstairs I catch a glimpse of somebody being hurriedly bustled out of the private office, and the great man himself comes to the door, smiling, and as I take his outstretched hand I am remembering other times that he has forgotten.

In the end—to make a long story short, as the saying is—Mr. Tuer, of "Ye Leadenhall Press," urged thereto by a mutual friend, read the book, and, I presume, found merit in it, for he offered to publish it if I would make him a free gift of the copyright. I thought the terms hard at the time (though in my eagerness to see my name upon the cover of a real book I quickly agreed to them), but with experience, I am inclined to admit that the bargain was a fair one. The English are not a book-buying people. Out of every hundred publications hardly more than one obtains a sale of over a thousand, and, in the case of an unknown writer, with no personal friends upon the Press, it is surprising how few copies sometimes *can* be sold.

I am happy to think that in this instance, however, nobody suffered. The book was, as the phrase goes, well received by the public, who were possibly attracted to it by its subject, a perennially popular one. Some of the papers praised it, others dismissed it as utter rubbish; and then, fifteen months later, on reviewing my next book, regretted that a young man who had written such a capital first book should have followed it up by so wretched a second.

One writer—the greatest enemy I have ever had, though I exonerate him of all but thoughtlessness—wrote me down a "humourist," which term of reproach (as it is considered to be in Merrie England) has clung to me ever since, so that now, if I pen a pathetic story, the reviewer calls it "depressing humour," and if I tell a tragic story, he says it is "false humour," and, quoting the dying speech of the broken-hearted heroine, indignantly demands to know "where he is supposed to laugh." I am firmly persuaded that if I committed a murder half the book reviewers would allude to it as a melancholy example of the extreme lengths to which the "new humour" had descended.

"Once a humourist, always a humourist," is the reviewer's motto.

"And all things allowed for—the unenthusiastic publisher, the insufficiently appreciative public, the wicked critic," says my little pink friend, breaking his somewhat long silence, "what do you think of literature as a profession?"

I take sometime to reply, for I wish to get down to what I really think, not stopping, as one generally does, at what one thinks one ought to think.

"I think," I begin, at length, "that it depends upon the literary man. If a man think to use literature merely as a means to fame and fortune, then he will find it an extremely unsatisfactory profession, and he would have done better to take up politics or company promoting. If he trouble himself about his status and position therein, loving the uppermost tables at feasts, and the chief seats in public places, and greetings in the markets, and to be called of men, Master, Master, then he will find it a profession fuller than most professions of petty jealousy, of little spite, of foolish hating and foolish log-rolling, of feminine narrowness and childish querulousness. If he think too much of his prices per thousand words, he will find it a degrading profession; as the solicitor, thinking only of his bills-of-cost, will find the law degrading; as the doctor, working only for two-guinea fees, will find medicine degrading; as the priest, with his eyes ever fixed on the bishop's mitre, will find Christianity degrading."

"But if he love his work for the work's sake, if he remain child enough to be fascinated with his own fancies, to laugh at his own jests, to grieve at his own pathos, to weep at his own tragedy—then, as, smoking his pipe, he watches the shadows of his brain coming and going before his half-closed eyes, listens to their voices in the air about him, he will thank God for making him a literary man. To such a one, it seems to me, literature must prove ennobling. Of all professions it is the one compelling a man to use whatever brain he has to its fullest and widest. With one or two other callings, it invites him—nay, compels him—to turn from the clamour of the passing day to speak for a while with the voices that are eternal.

"To me it seems that if anything outside oneself can help one, the service of literature must strengthen and purify a man. Thinking of his heroine's failings, of his villain's virtues, may he not grow more tolerant of all things, kinder thinking towards man and woman? From the sorrow that he dreams, may he not learn sympathy with the sorrow that he sees? May not his own brave puppets teach him how a man should live and die?

"To the literary man, all life is a book. The sparrow on the telegraph wire chirps cheeky nonsense to him as he passes by. The urchin's face beneath the gas lamp tells him a story, sometimes merry, sometimes sad. Fog and sunshine have their voices for him.

"Nor can I see, even from the most worldly and business-like point of view, that the modern man of letters has cause of complaint. The old Grub Street days when he starved or begged are gone. Thanks to the men who have braved sneers and misrepresentation in unthanked championship of his plain rights, he is now in a position of dignified independence; and if he cannot attain to the twenty thousand a year prizes of the fashionable Q.C. or M.D., he does not have to wait their time for his success, while what he can and does earn is amply sufficient for all that a man of sense need desire. His calling is a password into all ranks. In all circles he is honoured. He enjoys the luxury of a power and influence that many a prime minister might envy.

"There is still a last prize in the gift of literature that needs no sentimentalist to appreciate. In a drawer of my desk lies a pile of letters, of which if I were not very proud I should be something more or less than human. They have come to me from the uttermost parts of the earth, from the streets near at hand. Some are penned in the stiff phraseology taught when old fashions were new, some in the free and easy colloquialism of the rising generation. Some, written on sick beds, are scrawled in pencil. Some, written by hands unfamiliar with the English language, are weirdly constructed. Some are crested, some are smeared. Some are learned, some are ill-spelled. In different ways they tell me that, here and there, I have brought to someone a smile or pleasant thought; that to someone in pain and in sorrow I have given a moment's laugh."

PINKY YAWNS (OR A SHADOW thrown by the guttering candle makes it seem so). "Well," he says, "are we finished? Have we talked about ourselves, glorified our profession, and annihilated our enemies to our entire satisfaction? Because, if so, you might put me back. I'm feeling sleepy."

I reach out my hand, and take him up by his wide, flat waist. As I draw him towards me, his little legs vanish into his squat body, the twinkling eye becomes dull and lifeless. The dawn steals in upon him, for I have sat working long into the night, and I see that he is only a little shilling book bound in pink paper. Wondering whether our talk together has been as good as at the time I thought it, or whether he has led me into making a fool of myself, I replace him in his corner.

"Cavalry Life"

By "John Strange Winter"
(Mrs. Arthur Stannard)

My first book "as ever was" was written, or, to speak quite correctly, was printed, on the nursery floor some thirty odd years ago. I remember the making of the book very well; the leaves were made from an old copybook, and the back was a piece of stiff paper, sewed in place and carefully cut down to the right size. So far as I remember, it was about three soldiers and a pig. I don't quite know how the pig came in, but that is a mere detail. I have no data to go upon (as I did not dream thirty years ago that I should ever be so known to fame as to be asked to write the true history of my first book), but I have a wonderful memory, and to the best of my recollection it was, as I say, about three soldiers and a pig.

It never saw the light, and there are times when I feel thankful to a gracious Providence that I have been spared the power of gratifying the temptation to give birth to those early efforts, after the manner of Sir Edwin Landseer and that pathetic little childish drawing of two sheep, which is to be seen at provincial exhibitions of pictures, for the encouragement and example of the rising generation.

So far as I can recall, I made no efforts for some years to woo fickle fortune after the attempt to recount the story of the three soldiers and a pig; but when I was about fourteen my heart was fired by the example of a schoolfellow, one Josephine H——, who spent a large portion of her time writing stories, or, as our schoolmistress put it, wasting time and spoiling paper. All the same, Josephine H——'s stories were very good, and I have often wondered since those days whether she, in after life, went on with her favourite pursuits. I have never heard of her again except once, and then somebody told me that she had married a clergyman, and lived at West Hartlepool. Yes, all this has something to do, and very materially, with the story of my first book. For in emulating Josephine H——, whom I was very fond of, and whom I admired immensely, I discovered that I could write myself, or at least that I wanted to write, and that I had ideas that I wanted to see on paper. Without that gentle stimulant, however, I might never have found out that I might one day be able to do something in the same way myself.

My next try was at a joint story—a story written by three girls, myself and two friends. That was in the same year. We really made considerable headway with that story; and had visions of completely finishing it and getting no less a sum than thirty pounds for it. I have a sort of an idea that I supplied most of the framework for the story, and that the elder of my collaborators filled in the millinery and the love-making. But—alas for the futility of human hopes and desires!—that book was destined never to be finished, for I had a violent quarrel with my collaborators, and we have never spoken to each other from that day to this.

So came to an untimely end my second serious attempt at writing a book; for the stories that I had written in emulation of Josephine H——— were only short ones, and were mostly unfinished.

I wasted a terrible deal of paper between my second try and my seventeenth birthday, and I believe that I was, at that time, one of the most hopeless trials of my father's life. He many times offered to provide me with as much cheap paper as I liked to have; but cheap paper did not satisfy my artistic soul, for I always liked the best of everything. Good paper was my weakness—as it was his—and I used it, or wasted it, which you will, with just the same lavish hand as I had done aforetime.

When I was seventeen, I did a skit on a little book called "How to Live on Sixpence a Day." It was my first soldier story—excepting the original three soldiers and a pig—and introduced the "sixpence a day" pamphlet into a smart cavalry regiment, whose officers were in various degrees of debt and difficulty, and every man was a barefaced portrait, without the smallest attempt at concealment of his identity. Eventually this sketch was printed in a York paper, and the honour of seeing myself in print was considered enough reward for me. I, on the contrary, had no such pure love of fame. I had done what I considered a very smart sketch, and I thought it well worth payment of some kind, which it certainly was.

After this, I spent a year abroad, improving my mind—and I think, on the whole, it will be best to draw a veil over that portion of my literary history, for I went out to dinner on every possible occasion, and had a good time generally. Stay—did I not say my literary history? Well, that year had a good deal to do with my literary history, for I wrote stories most of the time, during a large part of my working hours and during the whole of my spare time, when I did not happen to be going out to dinner. And when I came home, I worked on just the same until, towards the end of '75, I drew blood for the first time. Oh, the joy of that first bit of money—my first earnings! And it was but a bit, a mere scrap. To be explicit, it amounted to ten shillings. I went and bought a watch on the strength of it—not a very costly affair; a matter of two pounds ten and an old silver turnip that I had by me. It was wonderful how that one half-sovereign opened up my ideas. I looked into the future as far as eye could see, and I saw myself earning an income—for at that time of day I had acquired no artistic feelings at all, and I genuinely wanted to make name and fame and money—I saw myself a young woman who could make a couple of hundred pounds from one novel, and I gloried in the prospect.

I disposed of a good many stories in the same quarter at starvation prices, ranging from the original ten shillings to thirty-five. Then, after a patient year of this not very luxurious work, I made a step forward and got a story accepted by the dear old *Family Herald*. Oh, yes, this is really all relevant to my first book; very much so, indeed, for it was through Mr. William Stevens, one of the proprietors of the *Family Herald*, that I learned to know the meaning of the word "caution"—a word absolutely indispensable to any young author's vocabulary.

At this time I wrote a great deal for the *Family Herald*, and also for various magazines, including *London Society*. In the latter, my first "Winter" work appeared—a story called "A Regimental Martyr."

I was very oddly placed at this point of my career, for I liked most doing the "Winter" work, but the ordinary young-lady-like fiction paid me so much the best, that I could not afford to give it up. I was, like all young magazine writers, passionately desirous of appearing in book form. I knew not a single soul in the way connected with literary matters, had absolutely no help or interest of any kind to aid me over the rough places, or even of whom to ask advice in times of doubt and difficulty. Mr. William Stevens was the only editor that I knew to whom I could go and say, "Is this right?" or "Is that wrong?" And I think it may be interesting to say here that I have never asked for, or indeed used, a letter of introduction in my life—that is, in connection with any literary business.

Well, when I had been hard at work for several years, I wrote a very long book—upon my word, in spite of my good memory, I forget what it was called. The story, however, lives in my mind well enough; it was the story of a very large family—about ten girls and boys, who all made brilliant marriages and lived a sort of shabby, idyllic, happy life, somewhat on the plan of "God for us all and the devil take the hindermost." Need I say that it was told in the first person and in the present tense, and that the heroine was anything but good-looking?

I was very young then, and thought a great deal of my pretty bits of writing and those seductive scraps of moralising, against which Mr. Stevens was always warning me. Well, this very long, not to say spun-out, account of this very large family of boys and girls, did not happen to please the "readers" for the *Family Herald*—then my stay-by—so I thought I would have a try round the various publishers and see if I could not get it brought out in three volumes. Of course, I tried all the best people first, and very often, when I receive from struggling young authors (who know a great deal more about my past history than I do myself, and who frequently write to ask me the best and easiest way to get on at novel-writing, without either hard work, or waiting, or disappointment, because, if you please, my own beginnings were so singularly successful and delightful) the information that I have never known of any of their troubles, it seems to me that my past and my present cannot be the past and present of the same woman. Yet they are. I went through it all; the same sickening disappointments, the same hopes and fears; I trod the self-same path that every beginner must assuredly tread, as we must all in time tread that other path to the grave. I went through it all, and with that exceedingly long and detailed account of that large and shabby family, I trod the thorny path of publishing almost to the bitter end—ay, even to the goal where we find the full-blown swindler waiting for us, with bland looks and honeyed words of sweetest flattery. Dear, dear! many who read this will know the process. It seldom varies. First, I sent my carefully written MS., whose very handwriting betrayed my youth, to a certain firm which had offices off the Strand, to be considered for publication. The firm very kindly did consider it, and their consideration was such that they made me an offer of publication—*on certain terms*.

Their polite note informed me that their readers had read the work and thought very highly of it, that they were inclined—just by the way of completing their list for the approaching September, the best month in the year for bringing out novels—to bring it out, although I was, as yet, unknown to fame. Then came the first hint of "the consideration," which took the form of a hundred pounds, to be paid down in three sums, all to fall due before the day of publication. I worked out the profits which *could* accrue if the entire edition sold out I found that, in that case, I should have a nice little sum for myself of 180*l*. Now, no struggling young author in his or her senses is silly enough to throw away the chance of making 180*l*. in one lump. I thought, and I thought the whole scheme out, and I must confess that the more I thought about it, the more utterly tempting did the offer seem. To risk 100*l*.—and to make 180*l*! Why, it was a positive sin to lose such a chance. Therefore, I scraped a hundred pounds together, and, with my mother, set off for London, feeling that, at last, I was going to conquer the world. We did a theatre on the strength of my coming good fortune, and the morning after our arrival in town set off—in my case, at all events—with swelling hearts, to keep the appointment with the kindly publisher who was going to put me in the way of making fame and fortune.

I opened the door and went in. "Is Mr.——at home?" I asked. I was forthwith conducted to an inner sanctum, where I was received by the head of the firm himself. Then I experienced my first shock—he squinted! Now, I never could endure a man with a squint, and I distrusted this man instantly. You know, there are squints and squints! There is the soft uncertain squint feminine, which is really charming. And there is a particular obliquity of vision which, in a man, rather gives a larky expression, and so makes you feel that there is nothing prim and formal about him, and seems to put you on good terms at once.

And there is a cold-blooded squint, which makes your flesh creep, and which, when taken in connection with business, brings little stories to your mind—"Is anyone coming, sister Anne?" and that sort of thing.

Mr.——asked me to excuse him a moment while he gave some instructions, and, without waiting for my permission, looked through a few letters, shouted a message down a speaking-tube, and then, after having arranged the fate of about half-a-dozen novels by the means of the same instrument, he sent a final message down the tube asking for my MS., only to be told that he would find it in the top right-hand drawer of his desk.

As a matter of fact, all this delay, intended to impress me and make me understand what a great thing had happened to me in having won attention from so busy a man, simply did for Mr.——so far as I was concerned. Instead of impressing me, it gave me time to get used to the place, it gave me time to look at Mr.——when he was not looking at me.

Then, having found the MS., he looked at me and prepared to give me his undivided attention.

"Well," he said, with a long breath, as if it was quite a relief to see a new face, "I am very glad you have decided to close with our offer. We confidently expect a great success with your book. We shall have to change the title though. There's a good deal in a title."

I replied modestly that there was a good deal in a title. "But," I added, "I have not closed with your offer—on the contrary, I—"

He looked up sharply, and he squinted worse than ever. "Oh, I quite thought that you had definitely—"

"Not at all," I replied; then added a piece of information, which could not by any chance have been new to him. "A hundred pounds is a lot of money, you know," I remarked.

Mr.——looked at me in a meditative fashion. "Well, if you have not got the money," he said rather contemptuously, "we might make a slight reduction—say, if we brought it down to 75*l.*, solely because our readers have spoken so highly of the story. Now look here, I will show you what our reader says—which is a favour that we don't extend to everyone, that I can tell you. Here it is!"

Probably in the whole of his somewhat chequered career as a publisher, Mr.——never committed such a fatal mistake as by handing me the report on my history (in detail) of that very large family of boys and girls. "Bright, crisp, racy," it ran. "Very unequal in parts, wants a good deal of revision, and should be entirely re-written. Would be better if the story was brought to a conclusion when the heroine first meets with the hero after the parting, as all the rest forms an anti-climax. This might be worked up into a really popular novel, especially as it is written very much in Miss——'s style" (naming a then popular authoress whose sole merit consisted in being the most faithful imitator of the gifted founder of a very pernicious school).

I put the sheet of paper down, feeling very sick and ill. And the worst of it was, I knew that every word of it was true. I was young and inexperienced then, and had not *nous* enough to say plump out that my eyes had been opened, and that I could see that I should be neither more nor less than a fool if I wasted a single farthing over a story that must be utterly worthless. So I prevaricated mildly, and said that I certainly did not feel inclined to throw a hundred or even seventy-five pounds away over a story without some certainty of success. "I'll think it over during the day," I said, rising from my chair.

"Oh, we must know within an hour, at the outside," Mr.——said very curtly. "Our arrangements will not wait, and the time is very short now for us to decide on our books for September. Of course, if you have not got the money, we might reduce a little more. We are always glad, if possible, to meet our clients."

"It's not that," I replied, looking at him straight. "I have the money in my pocket; but a Yorkshire woman does not put down a hundred pounds without some idea what is going to be done with it."

"You must let me have your answer within an hour," Mr.——remarked briefly.

"I will," said I, in my most polite manner; "but I really must think out the fact that you are willing to knock off twenty-five pounds at one blow. It seems to me if you could afford to take that much off, and perhaps a little more, there must have been something very odd about your original offer."

"My time is precious," said Mr.——in a grumpy voice.

"Then, good morning," said I cheerfully.

My hopes were all dashed to the ground again, but I felt very cheerful, nevertheless. I trotted round to my friend, Mr. Stevens, who gave a whistle of astonishment at my story. "I'll send my head clerk round for your MS. at once," he said, "else you'll probably never see it again."

And so he did, and so ended my next attempt to bring out my first book.

After this I felt very keenly the real truth of the old saying, "Virtue is its own reward." For, not long after my episode with Mr.——, the then editor of *London Society* wrote to me, saying that he thought that as I had already had several stories published in the magazine, it might make a very attractive volume if I could add a few more and bring them out as a collection of soldier stories.

I did not hesitate very long over this offer, but set to work with all the enthusiasm of youth—and youth does have the advantage of being full of the fire of enthusiasm, if of nothing else—and I turned out enough new stories to make a very respectable volume.

Then followed the period of waiting to which all literary folk must accustom themselves.

I was, however, always of a tolerably long-suffering disposition, and possessed my soul in patience as well as I could. The next thing I heard was that the book had very good prospects, but that it would have its chances greatly improved if it were in two volumes instead of being in only one.

Well, youth is generous, and I did not see the wisdom of spoiling the ship for the traditional ha'porth of tar, so I cheerfully set to work and evolved another volume of stories, all of smart, long-legged soldiers, and with—as Heaven knows—no more idea of setting myself up as possessing all knowledge about soldiers and the Service than I had of aspiring to the Crown of the United Kingdom of Great Britain and Ireland. But, even then, I had need of a vast amount of patience, for time went on, and really my book seemed as far from publication as ever. Every now and then I had a letter telling me that the arrangements were nearly completed, and that it would probably be brought out by Messrs. So-and-so. But days wore into weeks, and weeks into months, until I really began to feel as if my first literary babe was doomed to die before it was born.

Then arose a long haggle over terms, which I had thought were settled, and to be on the same terms as the magazine rates—no such wonderful scale after all. However, my literary guide, philosopher, and friend thought, as he was doing me the inestimable service of bringing me out, that 20*l.* was an ample honorarium for myself; but I, being young and poor, did not see things in the same light at all. Try as I would—and I cannot lay claim to trying very hard—I could not see why a man, who had never seen me, should have put himself to so much trouble out of a spirit of pure philanthropy, and a desire to help a struggling young author forward. So I obstinately kept to my point, and said if I did not have 30*l.*, I would rather have all of the stories back again. I think nobody would credit today what that special bit of firmness cost me. Still, I would cheerfully have died before I would have given in, having once conceived my claim to be a just one. A bad habit on the whole, and one that has since cost me dear more than once.

Eventually, my guide and I came to terms for the sum for which I had held out, namely, 30*l.*, which was the price I received for my very first book, in addition to about 8*l.* that I had already had from the magazine for serial use of a few of the stories.

So, in due course, my book, under the title of "Cavalry Life," was brought out in two great cumbersome volumes by Messrs. Chatto & Windus, and I was launched upon the world as a full-blown author under the name of "Winter."

So many people have asked me why I took that name, and how I came to think of it, that it will not, perhaps, be amiss if I give the reason in this paper. It happened like this. During our negotiations, my guide suggested that I had better take some *nom de guerre*, as it would never do to bring out such a book under a woman's name. "Make it as real-sounding and non-committing as you can," he wrote, and so, after much cogitation and cudgelling of my brains, I chose the name of the hero of the only story of the series which was written in the first person, and called myself J. S. Winter. I believe that "Cavalry Life" was published on the last day of 1881.

Then followed the most trying time of all—that of waiting to see what the Press would say of this, my first child, which had been so long in coming to life, and had been chopped and changed, bundled from pillar to post, until my heart was almost worn out before ever it saw the light. Then, on January 14, 1882, I went into the Subscription Library at York, where I was living, and began to search the new journals through, in but faint hopes, however, of seeing a review of my book so soon as that; for I was quite alone in the world, so far as literary matters went. Indeed, not one friend did I possess who could in anyway influence my career, or obtain the slightest favour for me.

I remember that morning so well; it is, I think, printed on my memory as the word "Calais" was on the heart of Queen Mary. It was a fine, cold morning, and there was a blazing fire in the inner room, where the reviews were kept. I sat down at the table, and took up the *Saturday Review*, never dreaming for a moment that I should be honoured by so much as a mention in a journal which I held in such awe and respect. And as I turned over the leaves, my eyes fell on a row of foot-notes at the bottom of the page, giving the names of the books which were noticed above, and among them I saw—"Cavalry Life, by J. S. Winter."

For full ten minutes I sat there, feeling sick and more fit to die than anything else. I was perfectly incapable of looking at the notice above. But, at last, I plucked up courage to meet my fate, very much as one summons up courage to have a tooth out and get the horrid wrench over. Judge of my surprise and joy when, on reading the notice, I found that the *Saturday* had given me a rattling good notice, praising the new author heartily and without stint. I shall never, as long as I live, forget the effect of that, my first review, upon me. For quite half an hour I sat without moving, only feeling, "I shall never be able to keep it up. I shall never be able to follow it up by another." I felt paralysed, faint, crushed, anything but elated and jubilant. And, at last, through some instinct, I put my hand up to my head to find that it was cold and wet, as if it had been dipped in the river. Thank Heaven, from that day to this I have never known what a cold sweat was. It was my first experience of such a thing, and sincerely I hope it will be my last.

"CALIFORNIAN VERSE"

By Bret Harte

When I say that my "first book" was *not* my own, and contained beyond the title-page not one word of my own composition, I trust that I shall not be accused of trifling with paradox, or tardily unbosoming myself of youthful plagiary. But the fact remains that in priority of publication the first book for which I became responsible, and which probably provoked more criticism than anything I have written since, was a small compilation of Californian poems indited by other hands.

A well-known bookseller of San Francisco one day handed me a collection of certain poems which had already appeared in Pacific Coast magazines and newspapers, with the request that I should, if possible, secure further additions to them, and then make a selection of those which I considered the most notable and characteristic for a single volume to be issued by him. I have reason to believe that this unfortunate man was actuated by a laudable desire to publish a pretty Californian book—*his* first essay in publication—and at the same time to foster Eastern immigration by an exhibit of the Californian literary product, but, looking back upon his venture, I am inclined to think that the little volume never contained anything more poetically pathetic or touchingly imaginative than that gentle conception. Equally simple and trustful was his selection of myself as compiler. It was based somewhat, I think, upon the fact that "the artless Helicon" I boasted "was Youth," but I imagine it was chiefly owing to the circumstance that I had from the outset, with precocious foresight, confided to him my intention of not putting any of my own verses in the volume. Publishers are appreciative; and a self-abnegation so sublime, to say nothing of its security, was not without its effect.

We settled to our work with fatuous self-complacency, and no suspicion of the trouble in store for us, or the storm that was to presently hurtle around our devoted heads. I winnowed the poems, and he exploited a preliminary announcement to an eager and waiting Press, and we moved together unwittingly to our doom. I remember to have been early struck with the quantity of material coming in—evidently the result of some popular misunderstanding of the announcement. I found myself in daily and hourly receipt of sere and yellow fragments, originally torn from some dead and gone newspaper, creased and seamed from long folding in wallet or pocket-book. Need I say that most of them were of an emotional or didactic nature; need I add any criticism of these homely souvenirs, often discoloured by the morning coffee, the evening tobacco, or, Heaven knows! perhaps blotted by too easy tears! Enough that I knew now what had become of those original but never re-copied verses which filled the "Poet's Corner" of every country newspaper on the coast. I knew now the genesis of every didactic verse that "coldly furnished forth the marriage table" in the announcement of weddings in the rural Press. I knew now who had read—and possibly indited—the dreary *hic jacets* of the dead in their mourning columns. I knew now why certain letters of the alphabet *had* been more tenderly considered than others, and affectionately addressed. I knew the meaning of the "Lines to Her who can best understand them," and I knew that they had been understood. The morning's post buried my table beneath these withered leaves of posthumous passion. They lay there like the pathetic nosegays of quickly-fading wild flowers, gathered by school children, inconsistently abandoned upon roadsides, or as inconsistently treasured as limp and flabby superstitions in their desks. The chill wind from the Bay blowing in at my window seemed to rustle them into sad articulate appeal. I remember that when one of them was whisked from the window by a stronger gust than usual, and was attaining a circulation it had never known before, I ran a block or two to recover it. I was young then, and in an exalted sense of editorial responsibility which I have since survived, I think I turned pale at the thought that the reputation of some unknown genius might have thus been swept out and swallowed by the all-absorbing sea.

There were other difficulties arising from this unexpected wealth of material. There were dozens of poems on the same subject. "The Golden Gate," "Mount Shasta," "The Yosemite," were especially provocative. A beautiful bird known as the "Californian Canary" appeared to have been shot at and winged by every poet from Portland to San Diego. Lines to the "Mariposa" flower were as thick as the lovely blossoms themselves in the Merced Valley, and the Madrone tree was as "berhymed" as Rosalind. Again, by a liberal construction of the publisher's announcement, *manuscript* poems, which had never known print, began to coyly unfold their virgin blossoms in the morning's mail. They were accompanied by a few lines stating, casually, that their sender had found them lying forgotten in his desk, or, mendaciously, that they were "thrown off" on the spur of the moment a few hours before. Some of the names appended to them astonished me. Grave, practical business men, sage financiers, fierce speculators, and plodding traders, never before suspected of poetry, or even correct prose, were among the contributors. It seemed as if most of the able-bodied inhabitants of the Pacific Coast had been in the habit at sometime of expressing themselves in verse. Some sought confidential interviews with the editor. The climax was reached when, in Montgomery Street, one day, I was approached by a well-known and venerable judicial magnate. After some serious preliminary conversation, the old gentleman finally alluded to what he was pleased to call a task of "great delicacy and responsibility" laid upon my "young shoulders." "In fact," he went on paternally, adding the weight of his judicial hand to that burden, "I have thought of speaking to you about it. In my leisure moments on the Bench I have, from time to time, polished and perfected a certain college poem begun years ago, but which may now be said to have been finished in California, and thus embraced in the scope of your proposed selection. If a few extracts, selected by myself, to save you all trouble and responsibility, be of any benefit to you, my dear young friend, consider them at your service."

In this fashion the contributions had increased to three times the bulk of the original collection, and the difficulties of selection were augmented in proportion. The editor and publisher eyed each other aghast. "Never thought there were so many of the blamed things alive," said the latter with great simplicity, "had you?" The editor had not. "Couldn't you sort of shake 'em up and condense 'em, you know? keep their ideas—and their names—separate, so that they'd have proper credit. See?" The editor pointed out that this would infringe the rule he had laid down. "I see," said the publisher thoughtfully—"well, couldn't you pare 'em down; give the first verse entire and sorter sample the others?" The editor thought not. There was clearly nothing to do but to make a more rigid selection—a difficult performance when the material was uniformly on a certain dead level, which it is not necessary to define here. Among the rejections were, of course, the usual plagiarisms from well-known authors imposed upon an inexperienced country Press; several admirable pieces detected as acrostics of patent medicines, and certain veiled libels and indecencies such as mark the "first" publications on blank walls and fences of the average youth. Still the bulk remained too large, and the youthful editor set to work reducing it still more with a sympathising concern which the good-natured, but unliterary, publisher failed to understand, and which, alas! proved to be equally unappreciated by the rejected contributors.

The book appeared—a pretty little volume typographically, and externally a credit to pioneer book-making. Copies were liberally supplied to the Press, and authors and publisher self-complacently awaited the result. To the latter this should have been satisfactory; the book sold readily from his well-known counters to purchasers who seemed to be drawn by a singular curiosity, unaccompanied, however, by any critical comment. People would lounge into the shop, turn over the leaves of other volumes, say carelessly, "Got a new book of California poetry out, haven't you?" purchase it, and quietly depart. There were as yet no notices from the Press; the big dailies were silent; there was something ominous in this calm.

Out of it the bolt fell. A well-known mining weekly, which I here poetically veil under the title of the Red Dog *Jay Hawk*, was first to swoop down upon the tuneful and unsuspecting quarry. At this century-end of fastidious and complaisant criticism, it may be interesting to recall the direct style of the Californian "sixties." "The hogwash and 'purp'-stuff ladled out from the slop bucket of Messrs.—— & Co., of 'Frisco, by some lop-eared Eastern apprentice, and called 'A Compilation of Californian Verse,' might be passed over, so far as criticism goes. A club in the hands of any able-bodied citizen of Red Dog and a steamboat ticket to the Bay, cheerfully contributed from this office, would be all-sufficient. But when an imported greenhorn dares to call his flapdoodle mixture 'Californian,' it is an insult to the State that has produced the gifted 'Yellow Hammer,' whose lofty flights have from time to time dazzled our readers in the columns of the *Jay Hawk*. That this complacent editorial jackass, browsing among the dock and thistles which he has served up in this volume, should make no allusion to California's greatest bard, is rather a confession of his idiocy than a slur upon the genius of our esteemed contributor." I turned hurriedly to my pile of rejected contributions—the *nom de plume* of "Yellow Hammer" did *not* appear among them; certainly I had never heard of its existence. Later, when a friend showed me one of that gifted bard's pieces, I was inwardly relieved! It was so like the majority of the other verses, in and out of the volume, that the mysterious poet might have written under a hundred aliases. But the Dutch Flat *Clarion*, following, with no uncertain sound, left me small time for consideration. "We doubt," said that journal, "if a more feeble collection of drivel could have been made, even if taken exclusively from the editor's own verses, which we note he has, by an equal editorial incompetency, left out of the volume. When we add that, by a felicity of idiotic selection, this person has chosen only one, and the least characteristic, of the really clever poems of Adoniram Skaggs, which have so often graced these columns, we have said enough to satisfy our readers." The Mormon Hill *Quartz Crusher* relieved this simple directness with more fancy: "We don't know why Messrs.——— & Co. send us, under the title of 'Selections of Californian Poetry,' a quantity of slum-gullion which really belongs to the sluices of a placer mining camp, or the ditches of the rural districts. We have sometimes been compelled to run a lot of tailings through our stamps, but never of the grade of the samples offered, which, we should say, would average about 33-1/3 cents per ton. We have, however, come across a single specimen of pure gold evidently overlooked by the serene ass who has compiled this volume. We copy it with pleasure, as it has already shone in the 'Poet's Corner' of the *Crusher* as the gifted effusion of the talented Manager of the Excelsior Mill, otherwise known to our delighted readers as 'Outcrop.'" The Green Springs *Arcadian* was no less fanciful in imagery: "Messrs.——— & Co. send us a gaudy green-and-yellow, parrot-coloured volume, which is supposed to contain the first callow 'cheepings' and 'peepings' of Californian songsters. From the flavour of the specimens before us we should say that the nest had been disturbed prematurely. There seems to be a good deal of the parrot inside as well as outside the covers, and we congratulate our own sweet singer 'Blue Bird,' who has so often made these columns melodious, that she has escaped the ignominy of being exhibited in Messrs.——— & Co. 's aviary." I should add that this simile of the aviary and its occupants was ominous, for my tuneful choir was relentlessly slaughtered; the bottom of the cage was strewn with feathers! The big dailies collected the criticisms and published them in their own columns with the grim irony of exaggerated head-lines. The book sold tremendously on account of this abuse, but I am afraid that the public was disappointed. The fun and interest lay in the criticisms, and not in any pointedly ludicrous quality in the rather commonplace collection, and I fear I cannot claim for it even that merit. And it will be observed that the animus of the criticism appeared to be the omission rather than the retention of certain writers.

But this brings me to the most extraordinary feature of this singular demonstration. I do not think that the publishers were at all troubled by it; I cannot conscientiously say that *I* was; I have every reason to believe that the poets themselves, in and out of the volume, were not displeased at the notoriety they had not expected, and I have long since been convinced that my most remorseless critics were not in earnest, but were obeying some sudden impulse started by the first attacking journal. The extravagance of the Red Dog *Jay Hawk* was emulated by others: it was a large, contagious joke, passed from journal to journal in a peculiar cyclonic Western fashion. And there still lingers, not unpleasantly, in my memory the conclusion of a cheerfully scathing review of the book which may make my meaning clearer: "If we have said anything in this article which might cause a single pang to the poetically sensitive nature of the youthful individual calling himself Mr. Francis Bret Harte—but who, we believe, occasionally parts his name and his hair in the middle—we will feel that we have not laboured in vain, and are ready to sing *Nunc Dimittis*, and hand in our checks. We have no doubt of the absolutely pellucid and lacteal purity of Franky's intentions. He means well to the Pacific Coast, and we return the compliment. But he has strayed away from his parents and guardians while he was too fresh. He will not keep without a little salt."

It was thirty years ago. The book and its Rabelaisian criticisms have been long since forgotten. Alas! I fear that even the capacity for that Gargantuan laughter which met them, in those days, exists no longer. The names I have used are necessarily fictitious, but where I have been obliged to quote the criticisms from memory I have, I believe, only softened their asperity. I do not know that this story has any moral. The criticisms here recorded never hurt a reputation nor repressed a single honest aspiration. A few contributors to the volume, who were of original merit, have made their mark, independently of it or its critics. The editor, who was for two months the most abused man on the Pacific slope, within the year became the editor of its first successful magazine. Even the publisher prospered, and died respected!

"Dead Man's Rock"

By "Q."

I cherish no parental illusions about "Dead Man's Rock." It is two or three years since I read a page of that blood-thirsty romance, and my only copy of it was found, the other day, in turning out the lumber-room at the top of the house. Later editions have been allowed to appear with all the inaccuracies and crudities of the first. On page 116, Bombay is still situated in the Bay of Bengal, and may continue to adorn that shore. The error must be amusing, since unknown friends continue to write and confess themselves tickled by it; and it is stupid to begin amending a book in which you have lost interest. But though this is my attitude towards "Dead Man's Rock," I can still look back on the writing of it as on an amusing adventure.

It was begun in the late summer of 1886, and was my first attempt at telling a story on paper. I am careful to say "on paper," because in childhood I was telling myself stories from morning tonight. Tens of thousands of small boys are doing the same everyday in the year; but I should be sorry to guess how much of my time, between the ages of seven and thirteen, must have been given up to weaving these childish epics. They were curious jumbles; the characters (of which I had a constant set) being drawn indiscriminately from the "Morte d'Arthur," "Bunyan's Holy War," "Pope's Iliad," "Ivanhoe," and a book of Fairy Tales by Holme Lee, as well as from history; and the themes ranging from battles and tournaments to cricket, wrestling, and sailing matches. Anachronisms never troubled the story-teller. The Duke of Wellington would cheerfully break a lance with Captain Credence or Tristram of Lyonesse, and I rarely made up a football fifteen without including Hardicanute (whom I loved for his name), Hector (dear for his own sake) and Wamba (who supplied the comic interest and scored off Thersites). They were brave companions; but at the age of thirteen they deserted me suddenly. Or perhaps after reading Mr. Stevenson's "Chapter on Dreams," I had better say it was the Piskies—the Small People—who deserted me. They alone know why—for their pensioner had never betrayed a single one of their secrets—or why in these later times, when he sells their confidences for money, they have come back to help him, though more sparingly. Three or four of the little stories in

"Noughts and Crosses" are but translated dreams, and there are others in my notebook; but now I never compose without some pain, whereas in the old days I had but to sit alone in a corner or take a solitary walk and invite them, and they did all the work. But one summer evening I summoned them and met with no response. Without warning the tales had come to an end.

From my first school at Newton Abbot I went to Clifton, and from Clifton in my nineteenth year to Oxford. It was here that the old desire to weave stories began to come back. Mr. Stevenson's "Treasure Island" was the immediate cause. I had been scribbling all through my school days; had written a prodigious quantity of bad reflective poetry and burnt it as soon as I really began to reflect; and was now plying the *Oxford Magazine* with light verse, a large proportion of which was lately reprinted in a thin volume, with the title of "Green Bays." But I wrote little or no prose. My prose essays at school were execrable. I had followed after false models for a while, and when gently made aware of this by the sound and kindly scholar who looked over our sixth-form essays at Clifton, had turned dispirited and wrote scarcely at all. Though reading great quantities of fiction, I had, as has been said, no thought of telling a story, and so far as I knew, no faculty. The desire, at least, was awakened by "Treasure Island," and, in explanation of this, I can only quote the gentleman who reviewed my first book in the *Athenæum*, and observed that "great wits jump, and lesser wits jump with them." That is just the truth of it. I began as a pupil and imitator of Mr. Stevenson, and was lucky in my choice of a master.

The germ of "Dead Man's Rock" was a curious little bit of family lore, which I may extract from my father's history of Polperro, a small haven on the Cornish coast. The Richard Quiller of whom he speaks is my great grandfather.

"In the old home of the Quillers, at Polperro, there was hanging on a beam a key, which we as children regarded with respect and awe, and never dared to touch, for Richard Quiller had put the key of his quadrant on a nail, with strong injunctions that no one should take it off until his return (which never happened), and there, I believe, it still hangs. His brother John served for several years as commander of a hired armed lugger, employed in carrying despatches in the French war, Richard accompanying him as subordinate officer. They were engaged in the inglorious bombardment of Flushing in 1809. Some short time after this they were taken, after a desperate fight with a pirate, into Algiers, but were liberated on the severe remonstrances of the British Consul. They returned to their homes in most miserable plight, having lost their all, except their Bible, much valued then by the unfortunate sailors, and now by a descendant in whose possession it is. About the year 1812 these same brothers sailed to the island of Teneriffe in an armed merchant ship, but after leaving that place were never heard of."

Here, then, I had the simple apparatus for a mystery; for, of course, the key must be made to unlock something far more uncommon than a quadrant; and I still think it a capital apparatus, had I only possessed the wit to use it properly. There was romance in this key—that was obvious enough, and I puzzled over it for some weeks, by the end of which my plot had grown to something like this: A family living in poverty, though heirs to great wealth—this wealth buried close to their door, and the key to unlock it hanging over their heads from morning tonight. It was soon settled, too, that this family should be Cornish, and the scene laid on the Cornish coast, Cornwall being the only corner of the earth with which I had more than a superficial acquaintance.

So far, so good; but what was the treasure to be? And what the reason that stood between its inheritors and their enjoyment of it? As it happened, these two questions were answered together. The small library at Trinity—a delightful room, where Dr. Johnson spent many quiet hours at work upon his "Dictionary"—is fairly rich in books of old travel and discovery; fine folios, for the most part, filling the shelves on your left as you enter. To the study of these I gave up a good many hours that should have been spent on ancient history of another pattern, and more directly profitable for Greats; and in one of them—Purchas, I think, but will not swear—first came on the Great Ruby of Ceylon. Not long after, a note in Yule's edition of "Marco Polo" set my imagination fairly in chase of this remarkable gem; and I hunted up all the accessible authorities. The size of this ruby (as thick as a man's arm, says Marco Polo, while Maundevile, who was an artist, and lied with exactitude, puts it at a foot in length and five fingers in girth), its colour, "like unto fire," and the mystery and completeness of its disappearance, combined to fascinate me. No form of riches is so romantic as a precious stone with a heart in it and a history. I had only to endow it with a curse proportionate to its size and beauty, and I had all that a story-teller could possibly want.

But even a treasure hunt is a poor affair unless you have two parties vying for the booty, and a curse can hardly be worked effectively until you introduce the fighting element, and make destiny strike her blows through the passions—hate, greed, &c.—of her victims. I had shaped my story to this point: the treasure was to be buried by a man who had slain his comrade and only confidant in order to enjoy the booty alone, and had afterwards become aware of the curse attached to its possession. And the descendants of these two men were to be rivals in the search for it, each side possessing half of the clue. It was at this point that, like George IV, I invented a buckle. My buckle had two clasps, and on these the secret of the treasure was so engraved as to become intelligible only when they were united.

My plot had now taken something like a shape; but it had one serious defect. It would not start to walk. Coax it as I might it would not budge. Even the worst book must have a beginning—this reflection was no less distressing than obvious, for mine had none. And there is no saying it would ever have found one but for a lucky accident.

In the Long Vacation of 1885 I spent three weeks or a month at the Lizard pollacking and reading Plato. Knowing at that time comparatively little of this corner of the coast, I had brought one or two guide books and local histories in the bottom of my portmanteau. One evening, after a stiff walk along the cliffs, I put the "Republic" aside for a certain "History and Description of the Parish of Mullyon," by its vicar, the Rev. E. G. Harvey, and came upon a passage that immediately shook my scraps of invention into their proper places.

The passage in question was a narrative of the wreck of the "Jonkheer Meester Van de Wall," a Dutch barque, on the night of March 25, 1867. I cannot quote at length the vicar's description of this wreck; but in substance and in many of its details it is the story of the "Belle Fortune" in "Dead Man's Rock." The vessel broke up in the night and drowned every soul on board except a Greek sailor, who was found early next morning clambering about the rocks under cliff, between Polurrian and Poljew. This man's behaviour was mysterious from the first, and his evidence at the inquest held on the drowned bodies of his shipmates was, to say the least, extraordinary. He said: "My name is Georgio Buffani. I was seaman on board the ship, which belonged to Dordrecht. I joined the ship at Batavia, *but I do not know the name of the ship or the name of the captain*." Being shown, however, the official list of Dutch East Indiamen, he pointed to one built in 1854, the "Kosmopoliet," Captain König. He then told his story of the disaster, which there was no one to contradict, and the jury returned a verdict of "Accidentally drowned." The Greek made his bow and left the neighbourhood.

Just after the inquest Mr. Broad, Dutch Consul at Falmouth, arrived, bringing with him the captains of two Dutch East Indiamen then lying at Falmouth. One of them asked at once "Is it Klaas Lammerts's?" Being told that the "Kosmopoliet" was the name of the wrecked ship, he said, "I don't believe it. The 'Kosmopoliet' wouldn't be due for a fortnight, almost. It must be Klaas Lammerts's vessel." The vicar, who had now come up, showed a scrap of flannel he had picked up, with "6. K. L." marked upon it. "Ah!" said the Dutchman, "it must be so. It *must* be the 'Jonkheer.'" But she had been returned "Kosmopoliet" at the inquest, so there the matter rested.

"On the Friday following, however," pursues the vicar, "when Mr. Broad and this Dutch captain again visited Mullyon, the first thing handed them was a parchment which had been picked up meanwhile, and this was none other than the masonic diploma of Klaas van Lammerts. Here, then, was no room for doubt. The ship was identified as the 'Jonkheer Meester van de Wall van Puttershoek,' Captain Klaas van Lammerts, 650 tons register, homeward bound from the East Indies, with a cargo of sugar, coffee, spices, and some Banca tin. The value of the ship and cargo would be between 40,000*l.* and 50,000*l.*" It may be added that on the afternoon before the wreck, the vessel had been seen to miss stays more than once in her endeavour to beat off the land, and generally to behave as if handled by an unaccountably clumsy crew. Altogether, folks on shore had grave suspicions that there was mutiny or extreme disorder of some kind on board; but of this nothing was ever certainly known.

I think this narrative was no sooner read than digested into the scheme of my romance, now for some months neglected and almost forgotten. But the Final School of Literæ Humaniores loomed unpleasantly near, and just a year passed before I could turn my discovery to account. The following August found me at Petworth, in Sussex, lodging over a clockmaker's shop that looked out upon the Market Square. Petworth is quiet; and at that time I knew scarcely a soul in the place; but lovely scenery lies all around it, and on a hot afternoon you may do worse than stretch yourself on the slopes above the weald and smoke and do nothing. There is one small common in particular, close to the monument at the top of the park, and just outside the park wall, where I spent many hours looking across the blue country to Blackdown, and lazily making up my mind about the novel. In the end—it was sometime in September—I called on the local stationer and bought a large heap of superior foolscap.

A travelling waxwork company was unpacking its caravan in the square outside my window on the morning when I pulled in my chair and light-heartedly wrote "Dead Man's Rock (a Romance), by Q.," at the top of the first sheet of foolscap. The initial was my old initial of the *Oxford Magazine* verses, and the title had been settled on for sometime before. Staying with some friends on the Cornish coast, I had been taken to a picnic, or some similar function, on a beach, where they showed me a pillar-shaped rock, standing boldly up from the sands, and veined with curious red streaks resembling bloodstains. "I want a story written about that rock," a lady of the party had said; "something really blood-thirsty. 'Slaughter Rock' might do for the name." But my title was really borrowed from the Dodman, locally called Deadman, a promontory east of Falmouth, between Veryan and St. Austell bays.

I had covered two pages of foolscap before the brass band of the waxwork show struck up and drove me out of doors and along the road that leads to the railway station—the only dull road around Petworth, and chosen now for that very reason. A good half of that morning's work was afterwards torn up; but I felt at the time that the enterprise was going well. I had written slowly, but easily; and, of course, believed that I had found my vocation, and would always be able to write easily—most vain delusion! For in six years and a half I have recaptured the fluency of that morning not half-a-dozen times. Still, I continued to take a lively interest in my story, and wrote at it very steadily, finishing Book I. before my return to Oxford. It surprised me, though, that, for all my interest in it, the story gave me little or no emotion. Once only did I get a genuine thrill, and that was at the point where young Jasper finds the sailor's cap (p. 25), and why at this point more than another is past explaining. In later efforts I have written several pages with a shaking pen and amid dismal signs of grief; and, on revision, have usually had to tear those pages up. On the whole, my short experience goes against

si vis me flere, dolendum est
Primum ipsi tibi.

But if *on revision* an author is moved to tears or laughter by any part of his work, then he may reckon pretty safely upon it, no matter with how stony a gravity it was written.

Book I.—just half the tale—was finished then, and put aside. The Oxford Michaelmas Term was beginning, and there were lectures to be prepared; but this was not all the reason. To tell the truth, I had wound up my story into a very pretty coil, and how to unwind it was past my contriving. When the book appeared, its critics agreed in pronouncing Part I to be a deal better than Part II, and they were right; for Book II is little more than a violent cutting of half-a-dozen knots that had been tied in the gayest of spirits; and it must be owned, moreover, that the long arm of coincidence was invoked to perform a great part of the cutting. For the time, however, the unfinished MS. lay in the drawer of my writing-table; and I went back to Virgil and Aristophanes and scribbled more verses for the *Oxford Magazine*. None of my friends knew at that time of my excursion into fiction; but one of them possesses the acutest eye in Oxford, and, with just a perceptible twinkle in it, he asked me suddenly, one evening towards the end of Term, if I had yet begun to write a novel. The shot was excellently fired, and I surrendered my MS. at once, the more gladly because believing in his judgment. Next morning he asserted that he had sat up half the night to read it. His look was of the freshest, but he came triumphantly out of cross-examination, and urged me to finish the story. In my elated mood I would have promised anything, and set to work at once to think out the rest of the plot; but it was not until the Easter Vacation that I finished the book, in a farmhouse at the head of Wastwater.

Another friend was with me, who, in the intervals of climbing, put all his enthusiasm into Aristotelian logic while I hammered away at the "immortal product," as we termed it by consent. It was further agreed that he should abstain from looking at a line of it until the whole was written—a compact which I have not heard he found any difficulty in keeping. Indeed, there was plenty to occupy us both without the book. Snow lay thick on the fells that spring, and the glissading was excellent; we had found, or thought we had, a new way up the Mickledore cliffs; and Mr. Gladstone had just introduced his first Home Rule Bill, and made the newspapers (which reached us a day late) very good reading. However, the MS. was finished and read with sincere, if discriminating, approval, on the eve of our departure.

The next step was to find a publisher. My earliest hopes had inclined upon my friend, Mr. Arrowsmith, of Bristol, who (I hoped) might remember me as having for a time edited the *Cliftonian*; but the book was clearly too long for his "Railway Library," and on this reflection I determined to try the publishers of "Treasure Island." Mr. Lyttelton Gell, of the Clarendon Press, was kind enough to provide a letter of introduction; the MS. went to Messrs. Cassell & Co., and I fear the end of my narrative must be even duller than the beginning. Messrs. Cassell accepted the book, and have published all its successors. The inference to be drawn from this is pleasant and obvious, and I shall be glad if my readers will draw it.

It is the rule, I find, to conclude such a confession as this with a paragraph or so in abuse of the literary calling; to parade one's self before the youth of merry England as the Spartans paraded their drunken Helot; to mourn the expense of energies that in any other profession would have fetched a nobler pecuniary return. I cannot do this; at any rate, I cannot do it yet. My calling ties me to no office stool, makes me no man's slave, compels me to no action that my soul condemns. It sets me free from town life, which I loathe, and allows me to breathe clean air, to exercise limbs as well as brain, to tread good turf and wake up every morning to the sound and smell of the sea and that wide prospect which to my eyes is the dearest on earth. All happiness must be purchased with a price, though people seldom recognise this; and part of the price is that, living thus, a man can never amass a fortune. But as it is extremely unlikely that I could have done this in any pursuit, I may claim to have the better of the bargain.

Certain gentlemen who have preceded me in this series have spoken of letters as of any ordinary characteristic pursuit. Naturally, therefore, they report unfavourably; but they seem to me to prove the obvious. Literature has her own pains, her own rewards; and it scarcely needs demonstration that one who can only bring to these a bagman's estimate had very much better be a bagman than an author.

"Undertones" and "Idyls and Legends of Inverburn"

By Robert Buchanan

My first serious effort in literature was what I may call a double-barrelled one; in other words, I was seriously engaged upon two books at the same time, and it was by the merest accident that they did not appear simultaneously. As it was, only a few months divided one from the other, and they are always, in my own mind, inseparable, or Siamese, twins. The book of poems called "Undertones" was the one; the book of poems called "Idyls and Legends of Inverburn" was the other. They were published nearly thirty years ago, when I was still a boy, and as they happened to bring me into connection, more or less intimately, with some of the leading spirits of the age, a few notes concerning them may be of interest.

A word, first, as to my literary beginnings. I can scarcely remember the time when the idea of winning fame as an author had not occurred to me, and so I determined very early to adopt the literary profession, a determination which I unfortunately carried out, to my own life-long discomfort, and the annoyance of a large portion of the reading public. When a boy in Glasgow, I made the acquaintance of David Gray, who was fired with a similar ambition to fly incontinently to London—

> *The terrible City whose neglect is Death,*
> *Whose smile is Fame!*

and to take it by storm. It seemed so easy! "Westminster Abbey," wrote my friend to a correspondent; "if I live, I shall be buried there—so help me God!" "I mean, after Tennyson's death," I myself wrote to Philip Hamerton, "to be Poet Laureate!" From these samples of our callow speech, the modesty of our ambition may be inferred. Well, it all happened just as we planned, only otherwise! Through some blunder of arrangement we two started for London on the same day, but from different railway stations, and, until some weeks afterwards, one knew nothing of the other's exodus. I arrived at King's Cross Railway Station with the conventional half-crown in my pocket; literally and absolutely half-a-crown; I wandered about the Great City till I was weary, fell in with a Thief and Good Samaritan who sheltered me, starved and struggled with abundant happiness, and finally found myself located at 66 Stamford Street, Waterloo Bridge, in a top room, for which I paid, when I had the money, seven shillings a week. Here I lived royally, with Duke Humphrey, for many a day; and hither, one sad morning, I brought my poor friend Gray, whom I had discovered languishing somewhere in the Borough, and who was already death-struck through "sleeping out" one night in Hyde Park.* "Westminster Abbey—if I live, I shall be buried there!" Poor country singing-bird, the great Dismal Cage of the Dead was not for *him*, thank God! He lies under the open Heaven, close to the little river which he immortalised in song. After a brief sojourn in the "dear old ghastly bankrupt garret at No. 66," he fluttered home to die.

To that old garret, in these days, came living men of letters who were of large and important interest to us poor cheepers from the North: Richard Monckton Milnes, Laurence Oliphant, Sydney Dobell, among others, who took a kindly interest in my dying comrade. But afterwards, when I was left to fight the battle alone, the place was solitary. Ever reserved and independent, not to say "dour" and opinionated, I made no friends, and cared for none. I had found a little work on the newspapers and magazines, just enough to keep body and soul alive, and while occupied with this I was busy on the literary twins to which I referred at the opening of this paper. What did my isolation matter, when I had all the gods of Greece for company, to say nothing of the fays and trolls of Scottish Fairyland? Pallas and Aphrodite haunted that old garret; out on Waterloo Bridge, night after night, I saw Selene and all her nymphs; and when my heart sank low, the fairies of Scotland sang me lullabies! It was a happy time. Sometimes, for a fortnight together, I never had a dinner—save, perhaps, on Sunday, when a good-natured Hebe would bring me covertly a slice from the landlord's joint. My favourite place of refreshment was the Caledonian Coffee House in Covent Garden. Here, for a few coppers, I could feast on coffee and muffins—muffins saturated with butter, and worthy of the gods! Then, issuing forth, full-fed, glowing, oleaginous, I would light my pipe, and wander out into the lighted streets.

Criticisms for the *Athenæum*, then edited by Hepworth Dixon, brought me ten-and-sixpence a column. I used to go to the old office

---

* See the writer's *Life of David Gray*.

in Wellington Street and have my contributions measured off on the current number with a foot-rule, by good old John Francis, the publisher. I wrote, too, for the *Literary Gazette*, where the pay was less princely—seven-and-sixpence a column, I think, but with all extracts deducted! The *Gazette* was then edited by John Morley, who came to the office daily with a big dog. "I well remember the time when you, a boy, came to me, a boy, in Catherine Street," wrote honest John to me years afterwards. But the neighbourhood of Covent Garden had greater wonders! Two or three times a week, walking, black bag in hand, from Charing Cross Station to the office of *All the Year Round* in Wellington Street, came the good, the only Dickens! From that good genie the poor straggler from Fairyland got solid help and sympathy. Few can realise now what Dickens was then to London. His humour filled its literature like broad sunlight; the Gospel of Plum-pudding warmed every poor devil in Bohemia.

At this time, I was (save the mark!) terribly in earnest, with a dogged determination to bow down to no graven literary idol, but to judge men of all ranks on their personal merits. I never had much reverence for gods of any sort; if the superior persons could not win me by love, I remained heretical. So it was a long time before I came close to any living souls, and all that time I was working away at my poems. Then, a little later, I used to go o' Sundays to the open house of Westland Marston, which was then a great haunt of literary Bohemians. Here I first met Dinah Muloch, the author of "John Halifax," who took a great fancy to me, used to carry me off to her little nest on Hampstead Heath, and lend me all her books. At Hampstead, too, I foregathered with Sydney Dobell, a strangely beautiful soul, with (what seemed to me then) very effeminate manners. Dobell's mouth was ever full of very pretty Latinity, for the most part Virgilian. He was fond of quoting, as an example of perfect expression, sound conveying absolute sense of the thing described, the doggrel lines—

> *Down the stairs the young missises ran*
> *To have a look at Miss Kate's young man!*

The sibilants in the first line, he thought, admirably suggested the idea of the young ladies slipping along the banisters and peeping into the hall!

But I had other friends, more helpful to me in preparing my first twin-offering to the Muses; the faces under the gas, the painted women on the bridge (how many a night have I walked up and down by their sides, and talked to them for hours together), the actors in the theatres, the ragged groups at the stage doors. London to me, then, was still Fairyland! Even in the Haymarket, with its babbles of nymph and satyr, there was wonderful life from midnight to dawn—deep sympathy with which told me that I was a born Pagan, and could never be really comfortable in any modern Temple of the Proprieties. On other points connected with that old life on the borders of Bohemia, I need not touch; it has all been so well done already by Murger, in the "Vie de Bohème," and it will not bear translation into contemporary English. There were cakes and ale, pipes and beer, and ginger was hot in the mouth too! *Et ego fui in Bohemiâ!* There were inky fellows and bouncing girls, *then; now* there are only fine ladies, and respectable, God-fearing men of letters.

It was while the twins were fashioning, that I went down in summer time to live at Chertsey on the Thames, chiefly in order to be near to one I had long admired, Thomas Love Peacock, the friend of Shelley and the author of "Headlong Hall"—"Greekey Peekey," as they called him, on account of his prodigious knowledge of things and books Hellenic. I soon grew to love the dear old man, and sat at his feet, like an obedient pupil, in his green old-fashioned garden at Lower Halliford. To him I first read some of my "Undertones," getting many a rap over the knuckles for my sacrilegious tampering with Divine Myths. What mercy could *I* expect from one who had never forgiven "Johnny" Keats for his frightful perversion of the sacred mystery of Endymion and Selene? and who was horrified at the base "modernism" of Shelley's "Prometheus Unbound?" But to think of it! He had known Shelley, and all the rest of the demigods, and his speech was golden with memories of them all! Dear old Pagan, wonderful in his death as in his life. When, shortly before he died, his house caught fire, and the mild curate of the parish begged him to withdraw from the library of books he loved so well, he flatly refused to listen, and cried roundly, in a line of vehement blank verse, "By the immortal gods, I will not stir!"*

Under such auspices, and with all the ardour of youth to help, my Book, or Books, progressed. Meantime, I was breaking out into poetry in the magazines, and writing "criticism" by the yard. At last

---

* I have given a detailed account of Peacock in my *Look Round Literature*.

the time came when I remembered another friend with whom I had corresponded, and whose advice I thought I might now ask with some confidence. This was George Henry Lewes, to whom, when I was a boy in Glasgow, I had sent a bundle of manuscript, with the blunt question, "Am I, or am I not, a Poet?" To my delight he had replied to me with a qualified affirmative, saying that in the productions he had "discerned a real faculty, and *perhaps* a future poet. I say perhaps," he added, "because I do not know your age, and because there are so many poetical blossoms which never come to fruit." He had, furthermore, advised me "to write as much as I felt impelled to write, but to publish nothing"—at any rate, for a couple of years. Three years had passed, and I had neither published anything—that is to say, in book form—nor had I had any further communication with my kind correspondent. To Lewes, then, I wrote, reminding him of our correspondence, telling him that I *had* waited, not two years, but three, and that I now felt inclined to face the public. I soon received an answer, the result of which was that I went, on Lewes's invitation, to the Priory, North Bank, Regent's Park, and met my friend and his partner, better known as "George Eliot."

But, as the novelists say, I am anticipating. Sick to death, David Gray had returned to the cottage of his father, the handloom weaver, at Kirkintilloch, and there had peacefully passed away, leaving as his legacy to the world the volume of beautiful poems published under the auspices of Lord Houghton. I knew of his death the hour he died; awaking in the night, I was certain of my loss, and spoke of it (long before the formal news reached me) to a friend. This by the way; but what is more to the purpose is that my first grief for a beloved comrade had expressed itself in the words which were to form the "proem" of my first book—

Poet gentle hearted,
Are you then departed,
And have you ceased to dream the dream we loved of old so well?
Has the deeply-cherish'd
Aspiration perished,
And are you happy, David, in that heaven where you dwell?
Have you found the secret
We, so wildly, sought for,
And is your soul enswath'd at last in the singing robes
you fought for?

Full of my dead friend, I spoke of him to Lewes and George Eliot, telling them the piteous story of his life and death. Both were deeply touched, and Lewes cried, "Tell that story to the public"; which I did, immediately afterwards, in the *Cornhill Magazine*. By this time I had my Twins ready, and had discovered a publisher for one of them, *Undertones*. The other, *Idyls and Legends of Inverburn*, was a ruggeder bantling, containing almost the first *blank verse* poems ever written in Scottish dialect. I selected one of the poems, "Willie Baird," and showed it to Lewes. He expressed himself delighted, and asked for more. I then showed him the "Two Babes." "Better and better!" he wrote; "publish a volume of such poems and your position is assured." More than this, he at once found me a publisher, Mr. George Smith, of Messrs. Smith and Elder, who offered me a good round sum (such it seemed to me then) for the copyright. Eventually, however, after "Willie Baird" had been published in the *Cornhill*, I withdrew the manuscript from Messrs. Smith and Elder, and transferred it to Mr. Alexander Strahan, who offered me both more liberal terms and more enthusiastic appreciation.

It was just after the appearance of my story of David Gray in the *Cornhill* that I first met, at the Priory, North Bank, with Robert Browning. It was an odd and representative gathering of men, only one lady being present, the hostess, George Eliot. I was never much of a hero-worshipper, but I had long been a sympathetic Browningite, and I well remember George Eliot taking me aside after my first *tête-à-tête* with the poet, and saying, "Well, what do you think of him? Does he come up to your ideal?" He *didn't* quite, I must confess, but I afterwards learned to know him well and to understand him better. He was delighted with my statement that one of Gray's wild ideas was to rush over to Florence and "throw himself on the sympathy of Robert Browning."

Phantoms of these first books of mine, how they begin to rise around me! Faces of friends and counsellors that have flown forever; the sibylline Marian Evans with her long, weird, dreamy face; Lewes, with his big brow and keen thoughtful eyes; Browning, pale and spruce, his eye like a skipper's cocked-up at the weather; Peacock, with his round, mellifluous speech of the old Greeks; David Gray, great-eyed and beautiful, like Shelley's ghost; Lord Houghton, with his warm worldly smile and easy-fitting enthusiasm. Where are they all now? Where are the roses of last summer, the snows of yester year? I passed by the Priory today, and it looked like a great lonely Tomb. In those days, the house where I live now was not built; all up here Hampstead-ways was grass and fields. It was over these fields that Herbert Spencer and George Eliot used to walk on their way to Hampstead Heath. The Sibyl has gone, but the great Philosopher still remains, to brighten the sunshine. It was not my luck to know him *then*—would it had been!—but he is my friend and neighbour in these latter days, and, thanks to him, I still get glimpses of the manners of the old gods.

With the publication of my first two books, I was fairly launched, I may say, on the stormy waters of literature. When the *Athenæum* told its readers that "this was *poetry*, and of a noble kind," and when Lewes vowed in the *Fortnightly Review* that even if I "never wrote another line, my place among the pastoral poets would be undisputed," I suppose I felt happy enough—far more happy than any praise could make me now. Poor little pigmy in a cockle-boat, I thought Creation was ringing with my name! I think I must have seemed rather conceited and "bounceable," for I have a vivid remembrance of a *Fortnightly* dinner at the Star and Garter, Richmond, when Anthony Trollope, angry with me for expressing a doubt about the poetical greatness of Horace, wanted to fling a decanter at my head! It was about this time that an omniscient publisher, after an interview with me, exclaimed (the circumstance is historical), "I don't like that young man; he talked to me as if he was God Almighty, or *Lord Byron*!" But in sober truth, I never had the sort of conceit with which men credited me; I merely lacked gullibility, and saw, at the first glance, the whole unmistakable humbug and insincerity of the Literary Life. I think still that, as a rule, the profession of letters narrows the sympathy and warps the intelligence. When I saw the importance which a great man or woman could attach to a piece of perfunctory criticism, when I saw the care with which this Eminent Person "humoured his reputation," and the anxiety with which that Eminent Person concealed his true character, I found my young illusions very rapidly fading. On one occasion, when George Eliot was very much pestered by an unknown lady, an insignificant individual, who had thrust herself somewhat pertinaciously upon her, she turned to me and asked, with a smile, for my opinion. I gave it, rudely enough, to the effect that it was good for "distinguished people" to be reminded occasionally of how very small consequence they really were, in the mighty life of the World!

From that time until the present I have pursued the vocation into which fatal Fortune, during boyhood, incontinently thrust me, and have subsisted, ill sometimes, well sometimes, by a busy pen. I may, therefore, with a certain experience, if with little authority, imitate those who have preceded me in giving reminiscences of their first literary beginnings, and offer a few words of advice to my younger brethren—to those persons, I mean, who are entering the profession of Literature. To begin with, I entirely agree with Mr. Grant Allen in his recent avowal that Literature is the poorest and least satisfactory of all professions; I will go even further, and affirm that it is one of the least ennobling. With a fairly extensive knowledge of the writers of my own period, I can honestly say that I have scarcely met one individual who has not deteriorated morally by the pursuit of literary Fame. For complete literary success among contemporaries, it is imperative that a man should either have no real opinions, or be able to conceal such as he possesses, that he should have one eye on the market and the other on the public journals, that he should humbug himself into the delusion that book-writing is the highest work in the Universe, and that he should regulate his likes and dislikes by one law, that of expediency. If his nature is in arms against anything that is rotten in Society or in Literature itself, he must be silent. Above all, he must lay this solemn truth to heart, that when the World speaks well of him the World will demand the *price* of praise, and that price will possibly be his living Soul. He may tinker, he may trim, he may succeed, he may be buried in Westminster Abbey, he may hear before he dies all the people saying, "How good and great he is! how perfect is his art! how gloriously he embodies the Tendencies of his Time!"* but he will know all the same that the price has been paid, and that his living Soul has gone, to furnish that whitewashed Sepulchre, a Blameless Reputation.

For one other thing, also, the Neophyte in Literature had better be prepared. He will never be able to subsist by creative writing unless it so happens that the form of expression he chooses is popular in form (fiction, for example), and even in that case, the work he does, if he is to live by it, must be in harmony with the social and artistic *status quo*. Revolt of any kind is always disagreeable. Three-fourths of the success of Lord Tennyson (to take an example) was due to the fact that this fine poet regarded Life and all its phenomena from the standpoint of the English public school, that he ethically and artistically

---

* O those "Tendencies of one's Time"! O those dismal Phantoms, conjured up by the blatant Book-taster and the indolent Reviewer! How many a poor Soul, that would fain have been honest, have they bewildered into the Slough of Despond and the Bog of Beautiful Ideas!—R. B.

embodied the sentiments of our excellent middle-class education. His great American contemporary, Whitman, in some respects the most commanding spirit of this generation, gained only a few disciples, and was entirely misunderstood and neglected by contemporary criticism. Another prosperous writer, to whom I have already alluded, George Eliot, enjoyed enormous popularity in her lifetime, while the most strenuous and passionate novelist of her period, Charles Reade, was entirely distanced by her in the immediate race for Fame. In Literature, as in all things, manners and costume are most important; the hall-mark of contemporary success is perfect Respectability. It is not respectable to be too candid on any subject, religious, moral, or political. It is very respectable to say, or imply, that this country is the best of all possible countries, that War is a noble institution, that the Protestant Religion is grandly liberal, and that social evils are only diversified forms of social good. Above all, to be respectable, one must have "beautiful ideas." "Beautiful ideas" are the very best stock-in-trade a young writer can begin with. They are indispensable to every complete literary outfit. Without them, the short cut to Parnassus will never be discovered, even though one starts from Rugby.

"Treasure Island"

By Robert Louis Stevenson

It was far indeed from being my first book, for I am not a novelist alone. But I am well aware that my paymaster, the Great Public, regards what else I have written with indifference, if not aversion; if it call upon me at all, it calls on me in the familiar and indelible character; and when I am asked to talk of my first book, no question in the world but what is meant is my first novel.

Sooner or later, somehow, anyhow, I was bound to write a novel. It seems vain to ask why. Men are born with various manias: from my earliest childhood, it was mine to make a plaything of imaginary series of events; and as soon as I was able to write, I became a good friend to the paper-makers. Reams upon reams must have gone to the making of "Rathillet," "The Pentland Rising,"* "The King's Pardon" (otherwise "Park Whitehead"), "Edward Daven," "A Country Dance," and "A Vendetta in the West"; and it is consolatory to remember that these reams are now all ashes, and have been received again into the soil. I have named but a few of my ill-fated efforts, only such indeed as came to a fair bulk ere they were desisted from; and even so they cover a long vista of years. "Rathillet" was attempted before fifteen, "The Vendetta" at twenty-nine, and the succession of defeats lasted unbroken till I was thirty-one. By that time, I had written little books and little essays and short stories; and had got patted on the back and paid for them—though not enough to live upon. I had quite a reputation, I was the successful man; I passed my days in toil, the futility of which would sometimes make my cheek to burn—that I should spend a man's energy upon this business, and yet could not earn a livelihood: and still there shone ahead of me an unattained ideal: although I had attempted the thing with vigour not less than ten or twelve times, I had not yet written a novel. All—all my pretty ones—had gone for a little, and then stopped inexorably like a schoolboy's watch. I might be compared to a cricketer of many years' standing who should never have made a run. Anybody can write

---

* *Ne pas confondre.* Not the slim green pamphlet with the imprint of Andrew Elliott, for which (as I see with amazement from the book-lists) the gentlemen of England are willing to pay fancy prices; but its predecessor, a bulky historical romance without a spark of merit, and now deleted from the world.

a short story—a bad one, I mean—who has industry and paper and time enough; but not everyone may hope to write even a bad novel. It is the length that kills. The accepted novelist may take his novel up and put it down, spend days upon it in vain, and write not anymore than he makes haste to blot. Not so the beginner. Human nature has certain rights; instinct—the instinct of self-preservation—forbids that any man (cheered and supported by the consciousness of no previous victory) should endure the miseries of unsuccessful literary toil beyond a period to be measured in weeks. There must be something for hope to feed upon. The beginner must have a slant of wind, a lucky vein must be running, he must be in one of those hours when the words come and the phrases balance of themselves—*even to begin*. And having begun, what a dread looking forward is that until the book shall be accomplished! For so long a time, the slant is to continue unchanged, the vein to keep running, for so long a time you must keep at command the same quality of style: for so long a time your puppets are to be always vital, always consistent, always vigorous! I remember I used to look, in those days, upon every three-volume novel with a sort of veneration, as a feat—not possibly of literature—but at least of physical and moral endurance and the courage of Ajax.

In the fated year I came to live with my father and mother at Kinnaird, above Pitlochry. Then I walked on the red moors and by the side of the golden burn; the rude, pure air of our mountains inspirited, if it did not inspire us, and my wife and I projected a joint volume of logic stories, for which she wrote "The Shadow on the Bed," and I turned out "Thrawn Janet" and a first draft of "The Merry Men." I love my native air, but it does not love me; and the end of this delightful period was a cold, a fly-blister, and a migration by Strathairdle and Glenshee to the Castleton of Braemar. There it blew a good deal and rained in a proportion; my native air was more unkind than man's ingratitude, and I must consent to pass a good deal of my time between four walls in a house lugubriously known as the Late Miss McGregor's Cottage. And now admire the finger of predestination. There was a schoolboy in the Late Miss McGregor's Cottage, home from the holidays, and much in want of "something craggy to break his mind upon." He had no thought of literature; it was the art of Raphael that received his fleeting suffrages; and with the aid of pen and ink and a shilling box of water colours, he had soon turned one of the rooms into a picture gallery. My more immediate duty towards the gallery was to be showman; but I would sometimes unbend a little, join the artist (so to speak) at the easel, and pass the afternoon with him in a generous emulation, making coloured drawings. On one of these occasions, I made the map of an island; it was elaborately and (I thought) beautifully coloured; the shape of it took my fancy beyond expression; it contained harbours that pleased me like sonnets; and with the unconsciousness of the predestined, I ticketed my performance "Treasure Island." I am told there are people who do not care for maps, and find it hard to believe. The names, the shapes of the woodlands, the courses of the roads and rivers, the prehistoric footsteps of man still distinctly traceable up hill and down dale, the mills and the ruins, the ponds and the ferries, perhaps the *Standing Stone* or the *Druidic Circle* on the heath; here is an inexhaustible fund of interest for any man with eyes to see or twopence worth of imagination to understand with! No child but must remember laying his head in the grass, staring into the infinitesimal forest and seeing it grow populous with fairy armies. Somewhat in this way, as I paused upon my map of "Treasure Island," the future character of the book began to appear there visibly among imaginary woods; and their brown faces and bright weapons peeped out upon me from unexpected quarters, as they passed to and fro, fighting and hunting treasure, on these few square inches of a flat projection. The next thing I knew I had some papers before me and was writing out a list of chapters. How often have I done so, and the thing gone no further! But there seemed elements of success about this enterprise. It was to be a story for boys; no need of psychology or fine writing; and I had a boy at hand to be a touchstone. Women were excluded. I was unable to handle a brig (which the *Hispaniola* should have been), but I thought I could make shift to sail her as a schooner without public shame. And then I had an idea for John Silver from which I promised myself funds of entertainment; to take an admired friend of mine (whom the reader very likely knows and admires as much as I do), to deprive him of all his finer qualities and higher graces of temperament, to leave him with nothing but his strength, his courage, his quickness, and his magnificent geniality, and to try to express these in terms of the culture of a raw tarpaulin. Such psychical surgery is, I think, a common way of "making character"; perhaps it is, indeed, the only way. We can put in the quaint figure that spoke a hundred words with us yesterday by the wayside; but do we know him? Our friend with his infinite variety and flexibility, we know—but can we put him in? Upon the first, we must engraft secondary and imaginary qualities, possibly all wrong; from the second, knife in hand, we must cut away and deduct the needless arborescence of his nature, but the trunk and the few branches that remain we may at least be fairly sure of.

On a chill September morning, by the cheek of a brisk fire, and the rain drumming on the window, I began "The Sea Cook," for that was the original title. I have begun (and finished) a number of other books, but I cannot remember to have sat down to one of them with more complacency. It is not to be wondered at, for stolen waters are proverbially sweet. I am now upon a painful chapter. No doubt the parrot once belonged to Robinson Crusoe. No doubt the skeleton is conveyed from Poe. I think little of these, they are trifles and details; and no man can hope to have a monopoly of skeletons or make a corner in talking birds. The stockade I am told, is from "Masterman Ready." It may be, I care not a jot. These useful writers had fulfilled the poet's saying: departing, they had left behind them Footprints on the sands of time, Footprints which perhaps another—and I was the other! It is my debt to Washington Irving that exercises my conscience, and justly so, for I believe plagiarism was rarely carried farther. I chanced to pick up the "Tales of a Traveller" some years ago with a view to an anthology of prose narrative, and the book flew up and struck me: Billy Bones, his chest, the company in the parlour, the whole inner spirit, and a good deal of the material detail of my first chapters—all were there, all were the property of Washington Irving. But I had no guess of it then as I sat writing by the fireside, in what seemed the spring-tides of a somewhat pedestrian inspiration; nor yet day by day, after lunch, as I read aloud my morning's work to the family. It seemed to me original as sin; it seemed to belong to me like my right eye. I had counted on one boy, I found I had two in my audience. My father caught fire at once with all the romance and childishness of his original nature. His own stories, that every night of his life he put himself to sleep with, dealt perpetually with ships, roadside inns, robbers, old sailors, and commercial travellers before the era of steam. He never finished one of these romances; the lucky man did not require to! But in "Treasure Island" he recognised something kindred to his own imagination; it was *his* kind of picturesque; and he not only heard with delight the daily chapter, but set himself acting to collaborate. When the time came for Billy Bones's chest to be ransacked, he must have passed the better part of a day preparing, on the back of a legal envelope, an inventory of its contents, which I exactly followed; and the name of "Flint's old ship"—

the "Walrus"—was given at his particular request. And now who should come dropping in, *ex machinâ*, but Dr. Japp, like the disguised prince who is to bring down the curtain upon peace and happiness in the last act; for he carried in his pocket, not a horn or a talisman, but a publisher—had, in fact, been charged by my old friend, Mr. Henderson, to unearth new writers for *Young Folks*. Even the ruthlessness of a united family recoiled before the extreme measure of inflicting on our guest the mutilated members of "The Sea Cook"; at the same time, we would by no means stop our readings; and accordingly the tale was begun again at the beginning, and solemnly re-delivered for the benefit of Dr. Japp. From that moment on, I have thought highly of his critical faculty; for when he left us, he carried away the manuscript in his portmanteau.

Here, then, was everything to keep me up, sympathy, help, and now a positive engagement. I had chosen besides a very easy style. Compare it with the almost contemporary "Merry Men"; one reader may prefer the one style, one the other—'tis an affair of character, perhaps of mood; but no expert can fail to see that the one is much more difficult, and the other much easier to maintain. It seems as though a full-grown experienced man of letters might engage to turn out "Treasure Island" at so many pages a day, and keep his pipe alight. But alas! this was not my case. Fifteen days I stuck to it, and turned out fifteen chapters; and then, in the early paragraphs of the sixteenth, ignominiously lost hold. My mouth was empty; there was not one word of "Treasure Island" in my bosom; and here were the proofs of the beginning already waiting me at the "Hand and Spear"! Then I corrected them, living for the most part alone, walking on the heath at Weybridge in dewy autumn mornings, a good deal pleased with what I had done, and more appalled than I can depict to you in words at what remained for me to do. I was thirty one; I was the head of a family; I had lost my health; I had never yet paid my way, never yet made 200*l.* a year; my father had quite recently bought back and cancelled a book that was judged a failure: was this to be another and last fiasco? I was indeed very close on despair; but I shut my mouth hard, and during the journey to Davos, where I was to pass the winter, had the resolution to think of other things and bury myself in the novels of M. de Boisgobey. Arrived at my destination, down I sat one morning to the unfinished tale; and behold! it flowed from me like small talk; and in a second tide of delighted industry, and again at a rate of a chapter a day, I finished "Treasure Island." It had to be transcribed almost exactly; my wife was ill; the schoolboy remained alone of the faithful; and John Addington Symonds (to whom I timidly mentioned what I was engaged on) looked on me askance. He was at that time very eager I should write on the characters of Theophrastus: so far out may be the judgments of the wisest men. But Symonds (to be sure) was scarce the confidant to go to for sympathy on a boy's story. He was large-minded; "a full man," if there was one; but the very name of my enterprise would suggest to him only capitulations of sincerity and solecisms of style. Well! he was not far wrong.

"Treasure Island"—it was Mr. Henderson who deleted the first title, "The Sea Cook"—appeared duly in the story paper, where it figured in the ignoble midst, without woodcuts, and attracted not the least attention. I did not care. I liked the tale myself, for much the same reason as my father liked the beginning: it was my kind of picturesque. I was not a little proud of John Silver, also; and to this day rather admire that smooth and formidable adventurer. What was infinitely more exhilarating, I had passed a landmark; I had finished a tale, and written "The End" upon my manuscript, as I had not done since "The Pentland Rising," when I was a boy of sixteen not yet at college. In truth it was so by a set of lucky accidents: had not Dr. Japp come on his visit, had not the tale flowed from me with singular ease, it must have been laid aside like its predecessors, and found a circuitous and unlamented way to the fire. Purists may suggest it would have been better so. I am not of that mind. The tale seems to have given much pleasure, and it brought (or was the means of bringing) fire and food and wine to a deserving family in which I took an interest. I need scarcely say I mean my own.

But the adventures of "Treasure Island" are not yet quite at an end. I had written it up to the map. The map was the chief part of my plot. For instance, I had called an islet "Skeleton Island," not knowing what I meant, seeking only for the immediate picturesque, and it was to justify this name that I broke into the gallery of Mr. Poe and stole Flint's pointer. And in the same way, it was because I had made two harbours that the "Hispaniola" was sent on her wanderings with Israel Hands. The time came when it was decided to republish, and I sent in my manuscript, and the map along with it, to Messrs. Cassell. The proofs came, they were corrected, but I heard nothing of the map. I wrote and asked; was told it had never been received, and sat aghast. It is one thing to draw a map at random, set a scale in one corner of it at a venture, and write up a story to the measurements. It is quite another to have to examine a whole book, make an inventory of all the allusions contained in it, and with a pair of compasses, painfully design a map to suit the data. I did it; and the map was drawn again in my father's office, with embellishments of blowing whales and sailing ships, and my father himself brought into service a knack he had of various writing, and elaborately *forged* the signature of Captain Flint, and the sailing directions of Billy Bones. But somehow it was never "Treasure Island" to me.

I have said the map was the most of the plot. I might almost say it was the whole. A few reminiscences of Poe, Defoe, and Washington Irving, a copy of Johnson's "Buccaneers," the name of the Dead Man's Chest from Kingsley's "At Last," some recollections of canoeing on the high seas, and the map itself, with its infinite, eloquent suggestion, made up the whole of my materials. It is, perhaps, not often that a map figures so largely in a tale, yet it is always important. The author must know his countryside, whether real or imaginary, like his hand; the distances, the points of the compass, the place of the sun's rising, the behaviour of the moon, should all be beyond cavil. And how troublesome the moon is! I have come to grief over the moon in "Prince Otto," and so soon as that was pointed out to me, adopted a precaution which I recommend to other men—I never write now without an almanack. With an almanack, and the map of the country, and the plan of every house, either actually plotted on paper or already and immediately apprehended in the mind, a man may hope to avoid some of the grossest possible blunders. With the map before him, he will scarce allow the sun to set in the east, as it does in "The Antiquary." With the almanack at hand, he will scarce allow two horsemen, journeying on the most urgent affair, to employ six days, from three of the Monday morning till late in the Saturday night, upon a journey of, say, ninety or a hundred miles, and before the week is out, and still on the same nags, to cover fifty in one day, as may be read at length in the inimitable novel of "Rob Roy." And it is certainly well, though far from necessary, to avoid such "croppers." But it is my contention—my superstition, if you like—that who is faithful to his map, and consults it, and draws from it his inspiration, daily and hourly, gains positive support, and not mere negative immunity from accident. The tale has a root there; it grows in that soil; it has a spine of its own behind the words. Better if the country be real, and he has walked every foot of it and knows every milestone. But even with imaginary places, he will do well in the beginning to provide a map; as he studies it, relations will appear that he had not thought upon; he will discover obvious, though unsuspected, shortcuts and footprints for his messengers; and even when a map is not all the plot, as it was in "Treasure Island," it will be found to be a mine of suggestion.

THE END

A NOTE ABOUT THE BOOK

Some of the Victorian era's brightest literary stars contributed to this collection of reminiscences on the struggle and reward of publishing a first book. Alongside such indisputable masters as **Robert Louis Stevenson, Arthur Conan Doyle**, and **Rudyard Kipling**, we encounter lesser-known figures like **Israel Zangwill**, a son of Jewish immigrants from London who earned acclaim from novelist George Gissing and President Theodore Roosevelt for such works as *The Melting Pot* (1908) and *Children of the Ghetto: A Study of Peculiar People* (1892). **Marie Corelli,** despite being rejected by the literary establishment of her time, was a pioneering science fiction writer whose bestselling works were beloved by the British people and Royal Family alike. **Hall Caine** was a bestselling writer whose novels, short stories, and poems—often set on his native Isle of Man—made him the most financially successful writer of his day. **H. Rider Haggard**, an influential forerunner of the lost world genre of literature, was an English writer whose tales of high adventure—notably *King Solomon's Mines* (1885)—won him popularity around the world.

A NOTE FROM THE PUBLISHER

Spanning many genres, from non-fiction essays to literature classics to children's books and lyric poetry, Mint Edition books showcase the master works of our time in a modern new package. The text is freshly typeset, is clean and easy to read, and features a new note about the author in each volume. Many books also include exclusive new introductory material. Every book boasts a striking new cover, which makes it as appropriate for collecting as it is for gift giving. Mint Edition books are only printed when a reader orders them, so natural resources are not wasted. We're proud that our books are never manufactured in excess and exist only in the exact quantity they need to be read and enjoyed.

bookfinity™

Discover more of your favorite classics with Bookfinity™.

- Track your reading with custom book lists.
- Get great book recommendations for your personalized Reader Type.
- Add reviews for your favorite books.
- AND MUCH MORE!

Visit **bookfinity.com** and take the fun Reader Type quiz to get started.

Enjoy our classic and modern companion pairings!

 **Classic & Modern**

Printed in the USA
CPSIA information can be obtained
at www.ICGtesting.com
JSHW082336140824
68134JS00020B/1713